Frank'ly
Dickens

"Chesterton" p.11

Patricia A. Vinci

15 January 2005

Frank'ly

Dickens

A Pop Culture Myth
Reinvents Itself
From
Charles Dickens
To
Frank Sinatra

Patricia A. Vinci

To order additional copies of this book, contact:
Xlibris Corporation
1-888-795-4274
www.Xlibris.com
Orders@Xlibris.com
25952

CONTENTS

A Toast to Tangerine

in memory of

Charles John

and

Francis Albert

½ PRICE SAVINGS
+ FREE GIFT!
with your paid subscription

BUSINESS REPLY MAIL
FIRST-CLASS MAIL   PERMIT NO. 22   TAMPA FL

POSTAGE WILL BE PAID BY ADDRESSEE

REAL SIMPLE
PO BOX 64523
TAMPA FL 33664-4523

SAVE 50% PLUS FREE GIFT!

Subscribe now and enjoy a second year at HALF the regular subscription rate!

☐ **YES!** Send me REAL SIMPLE for 2 years (24 issues). I'll pay $2.39 an issue for the first year and **ONLY $1.19 an issue for the second year**, a 50% savings. Plus, I'll get *Getting Organized* — a 40-page guide — **FREE with my paid subscription!**

☐ Instead, send me 1 year (12 issues) at $2.39 an issue. I'll still get my **FREE GIFT upon payment!**

NAME (PLEASE PRINT)

ADDRESS   APT. NO.

CITY   STATE   ZIP

E-MAIL

☐ Payment enclosed.   ☐ Bill me later.

SMALL75

Real Simple Solutions
Getting Organized

04ISMIA3

For faster service, call 1-800-621-6633

Or visit realsimple.com/order

REALSIMPLE ®

REAL SIMPLE

life | home | body | you

How to save $5,000 this year: 17 fast easy strategies

Great hair for under $7

As good as a new: quick fixes for your walls, floors, closet

Casual pants to fit anyone

10 ingredients, 30 meals

I Could Write A Book

This book is made up of well-known stories taken from the lives of two famous men. The remarkable thing about these stories is that they relate these two men to each other by pure coincidence. How else could the fickle finger of fate point out such an uncanny comparison between Charles Dickens—the beloved nineteenth-century British author of *A Christmas Carol*, and Frank Sinatra—the twentieth-century Italian-American singer, movie star leader of the Rat Pack—and expect us to notice?

That fickle finger does more than just point to the comparisons—it beckons us to come hither and take a closer look beneath the surface to see another dimension of life. It invites you to peek into the realm of myth from whence all the stories of the world come and go. In order to participate, only one thing is required of you, and that is imagination.

*   *   *

Frank Sinatra was just like Charles Dickens. They may appear entirely different on the outside but they were remarkably alike on the inside. Not only were they the same personality type, their personal and professional lives followed a pattern that was woven with extraordinary coincidence, year by year, a century apart. The reason for this is that Frank Sinatra and Charles Dickens lived the same myth. I'm not speaking about the myth that Frank Sinatra's life and persona created—I call that *The My Way Myth*. That is the myth projected on to Sinatra by his adoring fans. What I'm speaking about here is the subjective myth that Frank Sinatra was born to live—the myth that would take him *all the way*—the same myth that Charles Dickens lived the century before him. I've called this *The Pop Culture Myth* and, like all myths, it reinvented itself from one man's life into another's.

What people today don't realize about Charles Dickens is that he was so much more than just a great writer. Dickens was the first great superstar of universal stature in popular culture, and like Frank Sinatra, he dominated the field of popular entertainment for most of the century that he lived in. Dickens had entertained the world from the pages of his books for many years before embarking on a sensational public reading career, performing in America, as well as in Europe. A versatile and gifted actor, Dickens, and his one-man shows, became *The Main Event* of the nineteenth century.

In beginning to compare Charles Dickens with Frank Sinatra, one immediately sees that each man achieved modest fame by the age of twenty-four. Within a few years, however, this fame would skyrocket and force them into an intense spotlight that would focus on them for the rest of their lives! They had each come on the scene at exactly the right time in history, when the soil was fertile for their particular genius; Dickens, when books became economically affordable to everyone, and Sinatra, when recorded sound allowed us to bring music, as well as his voice, into our homes. Advancements in technology enabled both men to become famous almost immediately all over the civilized world.

In each case, this was no ordinary fame. This was fame of mythic proportions that would last a lifetime and beyond. And, this is no ordinary myth. This is a great myth and, as such, it deserves serious attention. This myth involves not only two famous men, but also two countries, who each reigned as a world power in a different century, who were marked to lead the world into a new millennium as the global community that it has become today. Exactly what the underlying influence each man had in moving this myth to where it is today, can be found in closely examining the details of their extraordinary lives.

Because their lives were, and increasingly continue to be, an open book, Charles Dickens and Frank Sinatra serve as perfect models of observation in demonstrating how myth operates in the universe in a span of two centuries. That is the purpose of this book, along with my intention to communicate insights on life that I have personally experienced and perceive of as truth. At the very least, my hope is that these observations will provoke some serious thought on the subject of myth, and perhaps heighten awareness in many people so that they can more readily share in the mysteries of life that surround us, which can never be explained by science or purely rational thought. Only then can we begin to observe and to learn more on our own, rather than to always rely on being taught by someone else's ideas. This book is not for the literal minded. It is geared to those blessed with a more poetic turn of mind who see life in an imaginative way.

The connection between Charles Dickens and Frank Sinatra is an intuitive one and cannot be proven—it can only be observed. All of these stories come from previously published sources. There is no way to prove that they are all true, only accepted as such. This alone validates them, however, because they have now become a part of each man's personal myth.

There is quite a bit to learn and to question in comparing the lives of Charles Dickens and Frank Sinatra; not only about why they were born so uniquely gifted as artists, or why they experienced a lifetime of unabating fame and adulation; but also about the less obvious gift that each, in his own way, gave back to the world in return.

UNDERSTANDING DICKENS

But there can be no question of the importance of Dickens as a
human event in history; a sort of conflagration and transfiguration in
the very heart of what is called the conventional Victorian era; a naked

flame of mere natural genius, breaking out in a man without culture, without tradition, without help from historic religions or philosophies or from the great foreign schools; and revealing a light that never was on sea or land, if only in the long fantastic shadows that it threw from common things.

—G.K. Chesterton

Charles Dickens is most famous as a nineteenth-century author who wrote fifteen popular novels, as well as the timeless classic *A Christmas Carol.* What is less commonly known about Dickens is that he was also an outstanding journalist and magazine editor, who used his pen not merely to write books—he used it in other ways to help change the world. He did this in the hundreds of articles and essays that he wrote for newspapers and magazines throughout his lifetime. In the process, Dickens left behind a vivid picture of the nineteenth century in prose.

Born at the beginning of the Industrial Revolution, when the printed word became the first mass form of universal communication, Dickens watched the world he lived in rapidly change. His passionate nature would not allow him to be idle and ignore the increasing needs of society. There was no social injustice that escaped his attention. While many others wrote on social issues in the nineteenth century, no one came close to having the immense universal reading audience that Dickens had, nor did any other writer possess his unique power of communication. Dickens never failed to lure an audience with his powerful pen. He wasn't sprinkling stardust to effect change, he was sprinkling thoughts and peppering them with emotions.

Only by taking into consideration that everything begins with a thought and that, as Emerson said, "thoughts rule the world," can one begin to fathom the vast influence and importance of Charles Dickens. To limit this achievement to the nineteenth century would be a mistake. Even if we were to ignore all of his works but one, he would still have reached into the twentieth century and beyond with his message of universal truths in *A Christmas Carol.* There is no possible way to measure all of the good that has come from this one little book alone—

a book unique in the literature of the world. While we can never fully realize Charles Dickens's contribution to the world's society, we should recognize that society owes a great debt to him.

It's doubtful that, to this day, anyone has ever surpassed Charles Dickens's explosion into popular culture. His popularity never languished in his lifetime. At the time of his death, he was proclaimed *The Shakespeare of the Novel* and he was said to be the most famous man in the world.

Dickens's allotted time on earth was short—he lived only fifty-eight years. But, his creative genius for writing was such that, in that brief period of existence, he became not only one of the greatest novelists of all time but the definitive voice of the nineteenth century. His unique style of writing is characterized by an effortless flow that has been described as liquid prose. Charles Dickens raised the novel to a literary art form and influenced all great writers who came after him.

UNDERSTANDING SINATRA

What few people, apart from musicians, have ever seemed to grasp is that he is not simply the best popular singer of his generation, a latter-day Jolson or Crosby, but the culminating point in an evolutionary process which has refined the art of interpreting words set to music. Nor is there even the remotest possibility that he will have a successor. Sinatra was the result of a fusing of a set of historical circumstances, which can never be repeated.

—Benny Green
British broadcaster, Popular Music critic and historian

Frank Sinatra was the most famous singer of popular music in the twentieth century. He also had a vast influence over the entire field of contemporary entertainment. Achieving sudden, spectacular fame at an early age, Sinatra became the first singer-teen idol. His appeal to all ages, however, soon became apparent when his voice was heard throughout the world on radio during World War ll.

On August 14, 1943, two years exactly to the day before the war would end; Sinatra sang with the Los Angeles Philharmonic Orchestra in a concert at The Hollywood Bowl, amid public debate over whether popular music should be performed at a venue used reservedly for classical music. Sinatra's comments at the end of the show convinced everyone of the appropriateness of including pop singing at classical performance halls from that evening on. This may have been the first demonstration of Sinatra's forthrightness but it wouldn't be the last. With a lifelong concern for humanity, the singer was one of the first entertainers to speak out for civil rights as far back as the forties, and he continued to do so through decades of social and racial unrest. There is no way to measure just how much Frank Sinatra's outspokenness, with his worldwide audience listening, helped move our country forward in the twentieth century.

From the very beginning, Sinatra's voice had an unusual hypnotic appeal. In his early career with the Tommy Dorsey Orchestra, couples would often separate when dancing, saunter up to the microphone and surround him while he was singing. During the war years, his voice was a therapeutic tool that helped people to deal with the pain of separation and loss. Later, through his music, as he suffered his own personal crisis of separation and loss, he helped millions of other people work their way through their own similar feelings and deal with their psychological pain. This personal relationship with his listeners continued long after his vocal powers waned and, even in old age, Sinatra continued to attract new generations of listeners as fans.

Frank Sinatra raised popular music to a classical art and influenced all of the great singers who came after him. No other singer, however, would ever possess his unique power of communication or his individual style of singing that was characterized by effortless flow and described as liquid baritone. Many of his near two thousand recordings are considered definitive versions of the songs. Like Shakespeare, famous for his understanding of human nature and for infusing this understanding into his characters with perfect articulation, Sinatra had an in-depth understanding of human feelings and emotion. He was able to infuse this understanding into his singing with perfect articulation as no other singer could. He is our very own Shakespeare of Song and is now considered the curator of the Great American Songbook.

UNDERSTANDING MYTH

Myth is the song of the universe, the music of the spheres, it's the music that we dance to even though we don't know the tune.
—Joseph Campbell

Life is a moving picture. Never had this been more apparent than in the twentieth century when the advent of motion picture film enabled us to look back and actually see for ourselves how things are constantly in flux. Every decade has its own look. People are the same but the symbols (hairstyles, fashions, modes of transportation, architecture, etc.) are ever changing. Technology has clearly demonstrated what William Shakespeare told us four centuries ago—that "all the world's a stage and all the men and women merely players". There is no doubt that the show goes on, the question is just how experienced are the players? Do they each have one part to play in one lifetime, or do they keep coming back to play other parts in the world's myths?

This book of comparative stories, adapted from accounts of the lives of Charles Dickens and Frank Sinatra, addresses this issue of myth and is based on my personal experience and observation of coincidences that have occurred in my own life, as well as the subsequent learning that has attended them. This learning incorporates the 1st and 2nd law of Thermodynamics, as I understand it to apply also to psychic energy; Emerson's theory on Compensation; the Universal Law of cause and effect called Karma that is said to govern the physical world and possibly rebirth; Jungian depth psychology; Joseph Campbell's teachings on myth; the study of name and number symbology; cycles and patterns of psychological growth attendant on energies generated by planetary transits in the study of astrology, which lends credence to the most important aspect of myth transference, namely, traveling; and Richard Wilhelm's translation of *The Chinese Book of Life: The Secret of the Golden Flower,* which confirms my observation that coincidences are confirmatory experiences and a way that the Cosmos communicates with us. For more details on my myth theory please read the summary at the end of this book.

PROLOGUE

FAIRY TALE

I n the early nineteenth century, a new age was dawning—
it was the Industrial Age. The cosmos was in the process of
creating a new myth and the world would soon be plunged into the
darkness of transformation. What the world needed was someone to
carry the torch, to bring some light into the darkness, to help see it
through. That someone needed one thing—a voice. He would have to
know how to use this voice, as the time was ripe for it to be heard by
everyone, everywhere.

While the world was busy making myth, out of the darkness of the
soil of transformation, a flower bloomed in the form of a corresponding
myth that gave the world the voice that it needed.

*   *   *

In a fairy tale setting, on the seventh of February in 1812, the voice of the nineteenth century was born. On the night of his birth, his mother, like Cinderella, was forbidden to go to the Ball—convention forbid it! Her child was due to be born soon and confinement was the order of the day for expectant mothers. She, too, must have been hard pressed to find a dress to wear—at least one that would fit her in her late stage of pregnancy. Elizabeth Dickens, however, loved to party, and so it was that she attended the Ball and *could have danced all night.* Alas, she arrived home *just in time.* For, by the first stroke of midnight, she presented her husband with a son and, at the same time, presented the world with a great gift, naming him Charles Dickens.

Under the circumstances, it seems likely that it was music that helped to determine the timing of the birth of Charles Dickens. Like the Homeopathic medicine of that century, the vial that contained the medicine for an ailing world was shaken and succussed by the movement of the dance to music, infusing it with great energy and spirit. Music was an important ingredient in the unique recipe that would make a Charles Dickens, and it was music that would accompany him throughout his life, and continue full circle when he was laid to rest.

Many years later, from the darkness of that soil, another flower would bloom in the form of a corresponding myth for the century to follow, providing the world, once more, with what it needed most—another voice. Continuing the thread of music that ran through Dickens's life, this time the voice would be a musical one.

*   *   *

In the early twentieth century, once again, a new age was dawning—it was the Psychological Age. A new myth was being created and, as usual, it was born out of necessity when the whole civilized world was twice plunged into a darkness of suffering so vast and severe, the likes of which had never been known before! Out of the darkness of the soil of two World Wars, a flower bloomed in the form of a corresponding myth that would fill the world with a garden of verses, which were written about love and set to music. What was needed was someone to carry the torch so that this songbook could be interpreted and preserved for all time. That someone needed one thing—a voice. He would have to know how to use this voice; for once again the time was ripe for it to be heard by everyone, everywhere.

*   *   *

The First World War was already in progress, and Charles Dickens was dead for almost a half-century, by the time the torchbearer of the new myth arrived. In a scene right out of a Dickens novel, Frank Sinatra was born in an unheated cold-water flat, *in the wee small hours of the morning* of December 12 in 1915. The mother was small, the baby was large and the doctor was incompetent. After a difficult birth, the baby didn't appear to be breathing, and the doctor hastily pronounced him dead. Fortuitously, the baby's fairy godmother—his grandmother, Rose—stood by to lend a helping hand. No one can say if what happened at that moment was just good common sense on the part of Rose or if she had used magical powers to give this baby with the exceptional breath control his first initiation into the life that awaited him. She grabbed Frank Sinatra, held him under a faucet, and brought him back to life with a splash of ice-cold water!

*   *   *

Ironically, Charles Dickens had been in a habit of splashing his face with ice-cold water, every morning, to bring himself back to life after a sound sleep. Having been awakened from his very first sleep by an orchestra playing music, Dickens's birth setting is, strangely, a more appropriate prelude to the life of Frank Sinatra and vice versa.

With Dickens now laid to rest at the foot of the grave of George Frederick Handel, the great composer of music, the torch could be passed. Charles Dickens had *put his dreams away* and could now truly rest in peace. Or could he?

THE HOUSE I LIVE IN

G reat Britain was well on its way to becoming the new world power at the time of Charles Dickens's birth, just seven years after it had defeated Napoleon in the greatest sea battle in history, The Battle of Trafalgar. Lord Nelson, wounded in the battle, had died, but the symbol lived on. His ship—The HMS Victory—would be returned home to Portsmouth to its final resting berth, just a few blocks from 387 Mile End Terrace where Dickens was born in 1812.

Britain was engaged in war with the United States that year, and the city of Portsmouth was once again the center for ship movements for the duration of the conflict. For the rest of his life, Dickens would retain the memory of wartime and the hordes of sailors who filled the streets of the seaport town where he was born.

*   *   *

The United States, like Great Britain the century before, was on its way to becoming the new world power at the time of Frank Sinatra's birth in Hoboken, New Jersey in 1915. With World War I already in progress, Hoboken, like Portsmouth, England in 1812, had also become a center for ship movements for the duration of the conflict, with troops leaving for battle in Europe from its port. For the rest of his life, Sinatra would retain the memory of World War I ending and the hordes of people celebrating in the streets of the town where he was born.

*   *   *

Dickens's family would only live in Portsmouth for a short while, as his father worked for the Navy Pay Office and his job was frequently relocated. Well before he was of school age, Dickens's mother impressed on him the importance of education. It was from his mother, also, that Frank Sinatra learned the importance of education. It was their fathers, however, who would expose them to one of their most formative childhood experiences. Ironically, the experience would be almost exactly the same for each of them.

With this formative experience, Charles Dickens's life would once again cross paths with the spirit of the great Lord Nelson, when the family relocated to another Navy base near Rochester, England. Dickens's father would take him to The Mitre Inn, where the famous hero, Nelson, had often stayed. While there, Dickens would entertain the lively crowd by singing *duets* with his sister, *Frances*. His father would lift the small slip of a boy up onto a table, where he would sing in a high-pitched voice and make people laugh. Later in life, Dickens would remark at what a nuisance he must have been to the grownups called upon to admire him. The thought of his shrill little voice still rang in his ears and made him blush. Dickens eventually came to realize that this was how he had developed the performing side of his persona, as well as an intense drive and need for applause.

A century later, the pattern would repeat itself, when Frank Sinatra's father would bring his small son into his pub and sit him up onto a piano where he, too, would sing in a high-pitched voice and make people laugh. Someone once gave the boy money, teaching him early on that he could sing for his supper. Later in life, Sinatra also recalled what a nuisance he had been with his "horrendous voice, just terrible, like a siren, way up high" and acknowledged that the seed of his performance personality was planted there, as well as the intense drive and need for applause.

One day Sinatra would sing *duets* just as Dickens had once done with his sister Frances. It's very clear that Frank Sinatra wasn't the first of the two to start his performing career as a saloon singer!

*   *   *

The happiest years of Dickens's childhood were spent in Rochester, an intriguing town with an ancient castle and medieval cathedral, and the place that he would always consider his hometown. It was here that a small, easily overlooked circumstance would lead Charles Dickens to his most important life lesson. His Aunt Fanny had come to live with them when her husband, a naval lieutenant, was drowned at sea in Rio de Janeiro. Shortly after, she remarried, this time to an army surgeon with a grown son, whose name was James Lamert. Lamert, who lived with the Dickens family for just a short while, had an immense influence on the boy, instilling in him a lifelong enthusiasm for the theater and acting. It was in a branch of this profession that Dickens, as a famous author, would reinvent himself and extend his sensational early fame into later life.

This enchanted phase of Dickens's childhood abruptly ended when his father was transferred to London. Dickens, still in school, stayed behind to finish the term, while the family moved on. When he finally left for London, it was with *high hopes*, but what awaited him now was a symbolic coach journey on a drizzly, dreary day, that would take him a great distance, not in miles, but in life. The journey would span from his childhood to his initiation into adulthood. It was the Hero's Journey, and like everything else in his life, it came too swiftly and too soon!

*   *   *

When the family was finally settled in London, Dickens's older sister Frances was sent to live and study at The Royal Academy of Music, while Charles was left to fend for himself. There was no mention of school, or any other prospects, for the neglected and confused boy. Only James Lamert seemed to sense his loneliness and built him a toy theater to play with. Dickens was clueless to the fact that a crisis was approaching due to his parents neglect in paying their bills. The truth is, they never learned to live within their means, and they were sinking deeper and deeper into debt as a result. Change arrived with lightning speed when his father was arrested one day, and the family was taken off to live with him in the Debtor's Prison. Once again, James Lamert stepped in and took Dickens to the theater. This time, however, it was the theater of life. Still an adolescent, Charles Dickens was being prepared to have a major role in the play.

Lamert, in an attempt to help the family, secured work for the young Dickens in the new business he had started in a shoe-blacking factory. Despite the fact that he was totally unfit for the toils of life as a street urchin, on February 9, 1824, just two days after his twelfth birthday, Charles Dickens was initiated into the horrors of the Industrial Age. Living on his own in a solitary room, and earning just enough money for sustenance, the boy would get to see his family on Sundays only. In the evening, when the prison doors were locked behind him, Dickens was once again left alone on the streets, with no hope of this bad dream having a happy ending.

Dickens, disguising the fact that he came from a lower middle class background, was always well dressed. Wearing a snappy hat on his head, he carried himself as proudly as any little gentleman would. A sheltered boy, with few friends, Dickens suddenly found himself independent. Sent out to mingle with other boys, he is immediately awakened from his illusions when they, sensing his difference, teased, ridiculed and perhaps beat him up. Dickens would never entirely recover from the pain and the humiliation of this horrifying ordeal. More important, he never got over the lesson he learned from this experience. Although he never spoke about it willingly to anyone, the world has yet to stop benefiting from his experience. It was here, on the streets, that

Charles Dickens learned about poverty, illiteracy, tolerance and integration. As a person, he may not have felt a part of this world of poverty and deprivation, but as a human being he felt a part of its pain. It would be his job to see that the rest of the world would feel it too.

With this crucial life lesson learned, Dickens was now prepared for his future role as torchbearer of the Industrial Age, and the easily overlooked circumstance that had led to it was the drowning of his uncle, the naval lieutenant, off the coast of Rio de Janeiro. Without this pivotal event, his aunt would never have come to live with his family in Rochester; Charles Dickens would never have known James Lamert or the blacking factory; and the world may never have known Oliver Twist or Ebenezer Scrooge!

*   *   *

Practically the whole country would have been in Debtor's Prison (had it still existed) during the Great Depression, when the lower middle class, well-dressed boy named Frank Sinatra, complete with a snappy hat on his head and carrying himself like a little gentleman, emerged from his sheltered life as a lonely, only child. He too is immediately awakened from his illusions when he is let out onto the streets to mingle with other boys, who sensing his difference, teased, ridiculed and beat him up! Sinatra never got over the pain and the humiliation of this horrifying ordeal. More important, he never got over the lesson he had learned from it. It was here on the streets that Frank Sinatra, like Charles Dickens, learned about poverty, illiteracy, tolerance and integration and someday he would make sure the rest of the world would know about it too.

*   *   *

Initiation complete, the scene changes suddenly and dramatically when Charles Dickens's paternal grandmother dies, leaving the family an inheritance. The father's debt paid, he is released from debtor's prison and the young Dickens is released from the blacking factory! Sent briefly back to school, Dickens's formal education ends prematurely when he is about the same age as Frank Sinatra when he dropped out of high school. Their lack of formal education had little effect on either of them, as they were both naturally voracious readers who continued to educate themselves on their own.

Dickens's ambition was to become an actor but complications arose when he fell madly and hopelessly in love with a fetching, bright-eyed little blond named Maria Beadnell. Maria never really took Charles seriously, but wasn't averse to leading him on! In addition to being a little older than he, she had the advantage of coming from a family with a higher social standing. After a while, Maria went off to Paris, only to return completely indifferent toward him. Despite Dickens's desperate attempt to reconcile with her through mutual friend, Marianne Leigh, who acted as intermediary, nothing moved the girl. He and Maria were in a wedding together and she attended the beautiful party that his parents gave for him on his birthday. There was music and dancing and Dickens sang with Maria and her sister Anne. Finally managing a private moment with her, she called Dickens "a boy" and left soon afterward. Maria was just too sophisticated for the young man who seemed to be going nowhere.

*   *   *

A century later, the scenario repeats itself in Frank Sinatra's life when he falls madly in love with a girl named Marie Roemer. She too was a blond, a little older than Frank, and also came from a family with a higher social standing. Frank confided in their mutual friend, Lee, but to no avail. Frank and Marie were in a wedding together, and she later attended the beautiful party that his parents threw in his honor one New Year's Eve. There was music and dancing, and Marie and her friend *Mary Scott* sang with Frank Sinatra. After a while, Marie began dating an older guy who took her to off to New York in a fancy car. Marie was just too sophisticated for the young man who seemed to be going nowhere.

*   *   *

In a few years, both of these young ladies would see things a lot differently. By then, it would be too late. The young Dickens would eventually have his heart broken one more time, not by unrequited love, but by the sudden death of his beloved young sister-in-law who, ironically, was also named Mary Scott. But, for now, the young man who walked reluctantly away from that doomed relationship with Maria Beadnell, permanently wounded, was more determined than ever to succeed. Fate had stepped in and placed a thorn in his side that would keep him restless and moving for the rest of his life.

2

MR. SUCCESS

The world was rapidly changing right in front of Charles Dickens's eyes as he grew to maturity. The Industrial Revolution was in full swing and the transportation revolution was moving along hand and hand with it. Beginning his career as a newspaper reporter, Dickens traveled by fast coach all over England at 10 mph, the same rate the Romans had traveled centuries before. With the advent of trains just a few years later, Dickens would soon be traveling at the previously unheard of rate of 60 mph.

And Frank Sinatra, approaching puberty in 1927 when Charles Lindbergh made the first transatlantic flight in an airplane, was old enough to be caught up in the wonder and excitement of the advent of air travel, which would someday lend an exotic flavor to his lifestyle. But, just as Dickens remained nostalgic for the old coaching days, the nostalgia for the rail travel of his youth would haunt Frank Sinatra.

The rapid advance and change in movement is symbolic of the age each man lived in, as well as of the rapid transformation that occurred in their lives by the age of twenty-five. *From this moment on*, they would have the opportunity to invest enormous amounts of energy in their art. In the process, the parallels in their lives speed up as well.

*　　*　　*

The enterprising young Dickens continued working as a reporter, while still aspiring to a career as a stage actor. In his free time, he took acting lessons and was finally accepted for an audition with a famous stage manager. He planned to take his sister Frances with him to supply the background music, but on the day of the long-awaited audition he had to cancel it, because Charles Dickens had a cold. By the time he could reapply for another audition, Dickens had already established himself as a writer. For the rest of his life, he would satisfy this yearning to act by performing in private theatricals. If Dickens had not become famous as a great writer, he may still have become famous as a great actor. Fate had stepped in and prevented this from happening with a timely cold that has become known as the most fortunate cold in the history of English literature. It gave us not only the greatest novelist of all time, but a superb journalist and magazine editor who eventually changed the face of modern journalism.

*　　*　　*

A cold would also become a part of Frank Sinatra's literature when, at the pinnacle of his career, he had to cancel the taping of his monumental television special, *Sinatra: A Man and His Music* because of one. This event inspired Gay Talese's famous Esquire magazine article—*Frank Sinatra Had A Cold*—that is credited with also having changed the face of modern journalism.

*　　*　　*

Around *1834*, Dickens became an author after winning a contest of sorts, when the first essay he submitted to a magazine was accepted and appeared in print. Inspired by William Hogarth's famous satirical paintings of London street scenes, Dickens began writing satirical sketches of similar scenes under the pen name of Boz. While he wasn't paid for this work, his talent did not go unnoticed. Before long, he and his sketches made a name for themselves. They were later collected and, on his twenty-fourth birthday, published in book form as *Sketches by Boz*.

Two months later Dickens planned to be married. He had fallen in love, on the rebound, with the daughter of a music critic he worked with. It's easy to deduce from his letters to his "Dear *Mouse*" that he and Catherine Hogarth were an ill-fated pair and that this was no grand passion. Dickens would marry her in spite of it, unaware that at that very moment he was on the brink of fame so great that it would change his life forever.

*   *   *

A hundred years later, around *1934*, Frank Sinatra's career as a singer began when he won a singing contest. He wasn't paid very much, but his talent did not go long unnoticed. Sinatra also married while he was on the brink of fame so great that it would change his life forever in ways that he could never have dreamed of or imagined. There would be many other women in his life that, like Dickens, he would call his "mouse," but his one Grand Passion was waiting down the line.

*   *   *

Charles Dickens unknowingly entered into the world of academia on the morning of *February 10th* in 1836, when he received an unexpected visitor to his apartment. The man came *not as a stranger*, for Dickens, on opening the door, recognized him immediately. The very same man who had sold him the magazine that contained his first published essay was now standing in his doorway offering him a job!

The man, William Hall, was a partner in the new publishing firm of Chapman and Hall. Even though Hall didn't remember him, Dickens took this as a good omen. Hall, a little bird-like man, seemed to come as a messenger from the gods. He was there to offer Dickens the opportunity to write a book that would eventually become the groundbreaking sensation, *The Pickwick Papers*.

There was nothing modest about the twenty-four year old author's prophetic claim that Pickwick would be not only triumphant, but also immortal! In no time, Charles Dickens and his book were overnight sensations, with his reading audience quickly recognizing the quaint originality of the book that had appeal for just about everyone.

The time was right, the technology was right and the method was right. Advances in printing, along with the innovative idea to publish his novels in monthly serials, to be sold at the affordable price of just a penny a piece, provided the perfect soil for Dickens's genius to flower into the very first worldwide pop culture sensation.

*   *   *

It was also on the *10th of February* that Frank Sinatra finally entered into the world of academia when, in 1997, he received a call on that very day from Hofstra University in Long Island, New York, asking his approval of an Academic Conference being planned there to study his phenomenal career spanning six decades as a singing artist.

From the beginning, the twenty-four year old Sinatra, not one to feign modesty either, had prophetically announced to the big bird-like man named Harry James, who had come to hear Sinatra sing and offer him a job, that he would be the greatest singer ever! James also arrived unexpectedly, though *not as a stranger*, for Sinatra recognized the Bandleader's name immediately. Another messenger from the gods had arrived; this time to offer Frank Sinatra an opportunity to sing with one of the big bands.

Again, the time was right, the technology was right and the method was right. Advanced technology in recording sound, and the rapid development of radio that followed for use in communication during World War II, allowed for Sinatra's voice to be heard everywhere.

Recorded on single disks, like the monthly parts of Dickens's novels, Sinatra's records were not only affordable, they became almost indispensable, as people all over the world listened and became addicted to the sound of The Voice over war radio!

*   *   *

Visually, Dickens and Sinatra bear little resemblance to each other. On hearing them described, however, it's difficult to tell them apart. Dickens, as a young adult, was said to be extremely youthful looking, handsome, slim, of medium height, and dressed up to the height of fashion. His dark hair fell over his temple; his eyes were strikingly blue and he had a wonderful smile—just like Frank Sinatra! Paradoxically, some saw them as beautiful and others saw them as coarse.

Initially, people who met them were disappointed by their thickness of speech. Both men had big ears, and neither one was conventionally handsome; they were something decidedly better, each with a face that was "beaming with life." Energetic, high-strung, and emotional (both men were known to cry), they were also intuitive geniuses, each with a will of iron, who demanded perfection in everything.

They loved to play charades and engage in practical jokes with the male companions who constantly surrounded them. Each achieved fame as a gifted actor. Dickens frequently performed in amateur theatricals. As a young man, he loved to dress up in a sailor's suit and dance a sailor's hornpipe. Sinatra, as a young man, would appear in more than one film, dancing in a sailor's suit. When making films, Sinatra was known as "one-take Charlie", but it was Charlie Dickens who was the very first to dance in a sailor's suit! Hollywood may have merely been recording this aspect of his myth on celluloid, starring Frank Sinatra!

*   *   *

Dickens's history of publishers parallels Sinatra's history of recording companies. He had contracts with two other publishers before he settled on the new publishing firm of Chapman and Hall. Initially, Dickens used his favorite expression, "*capital,*" to describe them. In his disputes with his two former publishers, they were in the right and Dickens was in the wrong. Neither realized what they were up against in this young, upstart of a writer. Defying the law paid off for Dickens, who insisted from the start that "they can't make me write", and they didn't! It was great practice in negotiation. From that time on, Dickens would emerge victorious from every dispute, regardless of any legal barrier that stood in his way. Once his back was up about an injustice, he immediately took an uncompromising stance and would never give an inch. Still in his twenties, Charles Dickens knew what it was to have power, and he intuitively knew how to use it.

In time, the name Charles Dickens and the name of the new publishing firm of Chapman and Hall would become synonymous. He made their fortune, but eventually went on to break with them and, more or less, start his own business when he hired printers to publish his books. However, it was to his first "capital" publishers, Chapman and Hall, that Dickens would return to in the end.

* * *

His life once again following the same pattern, Frank Sinatra recorded for two major labels before he settled on the recently formed Capitol Records, the company that his name would soon become synonymous with. Sinatra made their fortune, but later, in a bitter break with them, announced, "they can't make me sing!" Unlike Charles Dickens, Frank Sinatra did sing. This is difficult to fathom because, just like Dickens, once Sinatra's back was up about some injustice, he immediately took an uncompromising stance and would never give an inch.

Sinatra also went on to start his own company, but in the very end he returned to Capitol Records to record his last two *Duets* albums. Having come full circle, Frank Sinatra ended his performing career the very same way that Dickens began his—by singing duets!

If there is any doubt that Chapman and Hall's myth reinvented itself in Capitol Records, one has only to look at one of the Sinatra albums that Capitol released while Sinatra was recording exclusively for his own company, Reprise. It may be *just one of those things*, but printed directly beneath the Capitol logo in one corner of the later Sinatra album covers are the words "Pickwick Series!"

*   *   *

While Dickens's success with Pickwick had been swift, it had not been all smooth sailing. The story was originally the idea of a famous illustrator. Illustrators were the featured artists in books, and authors secondary, because prior to photographs, people were hungry for images. Charles Dickens would be the one to change all that. In this particular case, he didn't like the illustrator's idea and had a better one. Arguments ensued between the publisher, the famous artist and the little-known writer. In the end, the persuasive young Dickens got to do it his way! The distraught artist, after completing the illustration that he was working on for the book, (ominously titled "The Dying Clown"), went home and killed himself.

Why Dickens would write a serious tale of a dying clown and insert it into his comic masterpiece, *The Pickwick Papers,* can only be conjectured. He did, however, love the circus and had a fascination for clowns. As a child Dickens had seen the famous clown, Joseph Grimaldi, perform live on stage. Later he edited Grimaldi's *Memoirs.*

*   *   *

It's obvious, from a black and white photograph of the young Sinatra, paintbrush in hand, in the process of painting a clown, that he too must have had a fascination for them. Staring into the camera for the photograph, it looks as if Sinatra is trying to tell us something. Another, perhaps even more telling photograph—this one in color—shows him holding another clown painting on his lap and, reminiscent of Charles Dickens, Frank Sinatra is wearing a sailor's hat!

Later in life, the song "Send in The Clowns" would be an unusual part of Sinatra's repertoire during concerts. One wonders if he ever realized that the roots of his fame were directly linked to the circus, because it was from the circus that Harry James emerged into his own fame (his father was the circus bandleader) and, in the process, discovered Frank Sinatra.

*   *   *

Just like books before Dickens's day, that featured pictures in preference to words, music in Sinatra's day featured the band before the singer. Sinatra, like Dickens, would change all that when he went out to perform on his own. His manager, George Evans, died while trying in vain to prevent Sinatra from doing it his own way, as did Dickens's Pickwick illustrator Robert Seymour. By some innate or inherited wisdom, Frank Sinatra, still in his twenties, also knew what it was to have power and he intuitively knew how to use it.

*   *   *

With the book's illustrator gone, and Dickens having not yet come into his own, the popularity of *The Pickwick Papers* still greatly depended on the illustrations. A new artist had to be found immediately! The moon and the stars must have been in proper alignment the day Chapman and Hall happened upon the perfect artist for the job. Hablot K. Browne was a quiet, burly man with bushy hair, who was even younger than Dickens. Browne's nom-de-plume, Phiz, was a clever match for Dickens's pen name, Boz. They worked exclusively together for a long period of time, until Dickens felt the need to move on and he began to use other illustrators. No other artist was ever as ideally suited as Phiz to aid Dickens in his innovative goal of creating something completely original.

On his part, Dickens was more than willing to put in enormous amounts of time and effort, helping Phiz with each illustration, to assure that each one portrayed exactly what was described in his text. Dickens himself carefully studied the characters, as well as every object in the setting of the etching, offering recommendations to Phiz to insure that each illustration was perfect. Never again would Dickens choose to work this closely with any other of his illustrators.

Dickens may have started at the top, but it was his collaboration with Phiz and his publisher, Chapman and Hall, that would leave no doubt in anyone's mind, that he was there to stay!

*   *   *

There is no riddle to solve in determining with whom the same thing happened to Frank Sinatra. Nelson *Smock* Riddle came on the scene at a time when Frank was in dire need of a new arranger for his comeback with Capitol Records. Younger than Frank, Riddle was a quiet, burly man with short cropped bushy hair, who worked together with Sinatra for a long period of time before Sinatra went on to use other arrangers. No other arranger was ever as ideally suited as Riddle to aid Sinatra in his innovative goal of creating something completely original. Sinatra worked closely with Riddle in every aspect of arranging and conducting the music to insure that every song was perfect. Never again would Sinatra work this closely with any of his other arrangers.

Sinatra may have started at the top, but it was his collaboration with Nelson Riddle, and Capitol Records, that would leave no doubt in anyone's mind, that he was there to stay!

Once more, the moon and the stars must have been in proper alignment on the day that the integration of this fated pair of men took place. On first hearing a playback of that day's two prophetically titled recordings "Don't Worry 'Bout Me" and "I've Got the World On A String," Sinatra yelled out "I'm back!"

Good luck was definitely coming his way, for at the very first Capitol recording session, held on April 2, Frank Sinatra recorded the song "I'm Walking Behind You (on your Wedding Day)." He may very well have been, for it was Charles Dickens's wedding anniversary!

3

NANCY

B y the time Pickwick ended, Dickens was already nine months into writing his next novel, *Oliver Twist*. He had also written a farce for the stage and, surprisingly, an operetta that included a lovely song for which he wrote the lyrics, called "Autumn Leaves."

Once again, music would accompany Dickens as he turned another bend in the road in his life's journey. With this first flush of fame, he was moving faster than ever. His success was so swift and extraordinary that the critics were predicting that he would drop down as fast as he shot up. Far from being concerned, Dickens was already planning his next book. Knowing that everyone was expecting more Pickwickian type humor and fun, he purposely set out to give his readers the exact opposite.

Dickens briefly considered calling the dark novel that he was about to write *Frank Foundling*; but he later decided on *Oliver Twist*. The welfare of homeless and abused children was a predominate concern for Dickens throughout his life and he was anxious to present the much apparent social issue of neglected children in an enhanced emotional light. In the story, fate takes the little orphaned boy, Oliver, from the workhouse to a wicked thieves den in London, meagerly compensating in the darkness by his encounter with the kindly Nancy, and later compensating more adequately in the light by his encounter with the equally kind-hearted Rose Maylie. The culminating horror of the book is the brutal murder of Nancy, which is Dickens's potent warning of where neglect of society's unwanted children can lead. The fact that Dickens, from the very start of his career, demonstrated that he could portray, as equally effective, the darkness as well as the light, was without doubt the first sign of his great and lasting genius.

* * *

It is the equally effective portrayal of the darkness as well as the light, in Sinatra's music, that distinguishes him from other singers and which was an early sign of his great and lasting genius. Like Dickens, Sinatra did not suppress darkness, but integrated it into his world-view, as well as into his art, using this heightened awareness to effect psychosocial change.

The welfare of children was also a predominate concern for Sinatra throughout his life. This is evident from his many benefit performances for children's charities over his long career, most noteworthy his World Tour for the Children in 1962. In his harvest years, Frank Sinatra, in the true spirit of Charles Dickens, established a home for neglected and abused children in Palm Springs, California.

That Oliver might have been called Frank is an ironic twist, because if there is one Dickens book that reflects what was closest to Frank Sinatra's heart, it is this one. A closer look at the book reveals the startling precedence of the coincidental name of Nancy in both men's lives.

Nancy, the unlikely heroine of the book, who is brutally murdered for attempting to help the homeless Oliver, became increasingly important later in Dickens's life when he included the controversial scene of her murder in the repertoire of his reading performances. Dickens realistically portrayed the scene with such great force, it stunned audiences and caused a sensation. Ladies swooned when Dickens read about Nancy! A century later they would swoon when Frank Sinatra sang about Nancy!

His portrayal of Nancy's murder affected Dickens's health so adversely that his doctor ordered him to stop performing the reading. By the time he finally did stop, it was too late. Not long after, Dickens collapsed on the 8th of June and died twenty-four hours later. But, to this very day, it is said that Nancy killed Dickens!

$$* \quad * \quad *$$

If February 7 had fallen on a Saturday in 1939 (this was the hundredth-anniversary year of the publication of *Oliver Twist),* Frank Sinatra would have married *Nancy Rose* Barbato on Charles Dickens's birthday (they married on Saturday, February 4). Their first child, also named Nancy, was born the following year, on June 8, the date that Dickens collapsed just before he died. For Sinatra, this birth signaled an auspicious occasion, for the beautiful song "Nancy," written in honor of his firstborn child, became a sensational hit and, to this very day, remains one of his signature songs.

Fame as a singer also awaited his daughter Nancy, and "Boots" (the same type of shoe that the character Nancy wore in the novel and that all Victorian ladies wore in Dickens's day) became her signature song! Nancy Sinatra wore boots while singing on her award-winning television special, *Movin' with Nancy.* Uncharacteristically, one of the songs she sang on that show was from the musical *Oliver!*

Is imagination really crazy or is our whole perspective just lazy?

$$* \quad * \quad *$$

Dickens was still moving like wild-fire when he began writing his third novel, *Nicholas Nickleby,* while he was still in the middle of writing his second, *Oliver Twist.* With two stories appearing in monthly numbers concurrently, and both selling more copies than ever, his publishers commissioned a painted portrait of Dickens from which an engraving would be made to use as a frontispiece for his new novel when it was published in book form. *The Nickleby Portrait*, as it is called, was the precursor of the 8 x 10 glossy celebrity photos of the twentieth century. Just twenty-seven years old, Charles Dickens had been at the top of the heap for three straight years, and now, not only could Dickens's voice be heard through his writing, but fans all over the world could see what he looked like too!

These first four years of fame were the most thrilling years of Dickens's life. His books were still the rage and his personal life was equally exciting. Settling into his first home with his wife and baby, he was invited to all of the famous London salons, where he met and formed friendships with literary men, artists, actors, politicians and other prominent people. Dickens was also offered memberships in London's most exclusive clubs; his biggest thrill being elected into England's most prestigious club, The Athenaeum; an honor that eluded many famous men until old age. His invitation to join the Garrick Club—the haunt of actors, as well as artists and literary men—put Dickens in touch with people he could more comfortably relate to.

Over the years, there would be a lot of controversy surrounding Dickens's membership in the Garrick Club. He would resign more than once, becoming estranged from people who were once dear to him, over the controversy, but whom he would later reconcile with. As a middle-aged man, the very last time Dickens resigned from the Garrick Club, it was over a scandal concerning a teenage actress he had fallen in love with.

*   *   *

The name Garrick became prominent very early in Frank Sinatra's life when he was accidentally baptized with the name Frank after his godfather (Frank Garrick) at his Christening. This event also took place on Charles Dickens's wedding anniversary on April 2, which definitely lends suspicion of added significance to this initiation rite in Sinatra's life.

Frank Garrick would one day secure for his godson, and namesake, his first job, working for a newspaper, where the young Sinatra aspired to be a reporter, just as Dickens had once been. When this job abruptly ended, Sinatra became estranged from Frank Garrick but he would later reconcile with him. One door closed, but another opened, as Frank Sinatra was hired for a new job, this time working with books! Instead of writing them, he would lift them, in heavy boxes, up onto a loading dock, under the direction of a Cockney supervisor.

*   *   *

It was around the time Dickens began writing Oliver that he formed a friendship with John Forster, the man who would become his closest friend and confidant. He and Dickens, opposites in many ways, warmed to each other immediately. An opinionated, sometimes overbearing bull of a man, who loved Dickens deeply, Forster proved to be a faithful friend. Fuzz, as he was jokingly referred to in literary circles, became a mental bodyguard for Dickens. Described as a human steamroller, he would step in and insure that Dickens be protected and receive all that he deserved in his conflicts with his publishers or anyone else.

It wasn't until later in life that Dickens would form another close friendship with a man who would also become a business associate/ bodyguard for him. Dickens hired George Dolby to manage his public reading performances. From the moment they met, Dickens and Dolby were instantly attracted to one another. Dolby, who devotedly called Dickens his "Chief", was a big, bald, incredibly thick-skinned man, who had a stock of jokes and a loud laugh.

*   *   *

In his long career, Sinatra also would have two close friends who were business associates, as well as bodyguards: Hank Sanicola, the human steam roller who supposedly helped extricate Sinatra from his iron clad contract with Tommy Dorsey; and later Jilly Rizzo. There was an instant attraction between Sinatra and Jilly, who with his stock of jokes and loud laugh would take the place of Dolby in Sinatra's life.

*   *   *

Dickens had a genuine need for friendship, and whenever he had any free time, he always spent it with one or more of his male companions, most of whom were his friends for life. His oldest friend was Tom Beard, who had worked with Dickens in his early reporter days and who had served as best man in his wedding. When Dickens became famous and had made many more influential friends, he would always remember *Tommy* and include him in the many exciting events of his fabulous life. Tom's brother, Frank Beard, would also become increasingly important in Dickens's life, as his attending physician. *Frank* would accompany Dickens when he performed his last public readings.

Frank Sinatra also had a genuine need for friendship and he, too, always surrounded himself with one or more male companions. It was to his old friend and mentor Tommy Dorsey, who he had worked for in his earliest days as a singer, that he gave credit for teaching him everything he needed to know. He chose Tommy to be godfather to his firstborn, Nancy, at her christening. Years later, Sinatra, getting sentimental over his past, recorded a special tribute album to Dorsey, telling the entire world *I Remember Tommy*.

*   *   *

With a career that allowed him to set his own working hours, Dickens was able to live on impulse. It wasn't unusual for his friends to receive a last-minute note asking them to join him on a horseback excursion to some pub, in the outskirts of London, to take in a pint of ale and a hot chop. At other times, it was an invitation to go even further on extended trips to places where Dickens could procure ideas for his books. When vacationing each year, he would rent a place that was large enough to accommodate not only his family, but also the many friends who were given an open invitation to join them.

With a career that allowed him to set his own working hours, Sinatra also was able to live on impulse. It wasn't unusual for his friends to receive a last-minute note asking them to join him on an airplane excursion and be sure to bring along their passport. You were never sure where you would end up with Sinatra, but there was no need to worry about bringing any clothes along with you for the trip. Sinatra would buy you new ones when you got there!

*   *   *

Of course, fate would insist on a dark moment in the midst of such a happy time in Dickens's life, and it would be a very dark one indeed. His seventeen year old sister-in-law, *Mary Scott* Hogarth, who had come to live with Dickens and his wife in their new home, died suddenly of heart failure while she lay in Dickens's arms. In shock and deep distress, Dickens removed the ring she wore and placed it on his little finger, where it stayed for the rest of his life. This ring and replicas of it are still worn by his descendants today.

And Frank Sinatra, who as a young man once sang at a party with another Mary Scott, also wore a ring, of special significance, on his little finger, that his children still wear replicas of today.

*   *   *

Once again it was darkness mingled with the light in Dickens's life that marked the two most wonderful and productive years that he lived in his first home at 48 Doughty Street in London. You can still visit there today and see where *Oliver Twist* and *Nicholas Nickleby* were written, and where his two daughters, Mary and Kate, were born. Shortly after, the family moved to a far grander house in Devonshire Terrace, and it was here that Dickens would create two more daughters, this time in his fictional family: Little Nell who, like Mary Scott Hogarth, would die and break everyone's heart in his fourth novel, *The Old Curiosity Shop*; and the lovely coquettish Dolly Varden, not unlike his first love Maria Beadnell, who would captivate readers in *Barnaby Rudge*. It was also at Devonshire Terrace that Dickens would create two of his most distinctive masterpieces: *A Christmas Carol* and *David Copperfield*. Before he would write these books, however, Charles Dickens would go off on a magnificent journey to America.

The New World was waiting for the beloved author of the books that had enthralled them. What Americans weren't prepared for was the fearlessly outspoken, eagle-eyed surveyor who would give America the jolt needed to help move it along toward the twentieth century.

4

MY SHINING HOUR

Once the idea had gotten into his head, Dickens became increasingly possessed by a desire to see the New World. Nothing would stop him—not his wife's tears, or the fact that he had little ones at home, or the inclement weather. With an advance from his publisher and an agreement to write a travel book, on the fourth day of January in 1842, Charles Dickens and his wife boarded the Britannia steamer in Liverpool, England and sailed off to America. After a horrendous eighteen-day sea passage, the ship finally arrived in Boston. As it approached the harbor, Dickens, standing on deck, was amazed to see what he thought was a crowd of newsboys "leaping aboard at the peril of their lives". The newsboys turned out to be reporters who immediately converged on him like savages. Caught unawares, the youthful twenty-nine year old Dickens had his first welcome to America! The celebrity of the century—forerunner of the pop-stars of the next—had just arrived and been given his first taste of what was in store for him.

Nothing, however, would deter the high-spirited Dickens as he burst through the doorway of the lobby of the Tremont House Hotel with the shout "Here we are!" That shout would echo throughout the entire land, as everywhere the author traveled, there were throngs of people waiting eagerly to see him. With thousands of outstretched hands to shake, autographs to sign, receptions, dinners and balls to attend, Dickens soon found the seemingly endless list of things expected of him to do intolerable.

Crowds lined the street in Boston, waiting to catch a glimpse of the famous author as he emerged from the hotel. He was forced to push his way through a surging mob in order to cross the street to the Tremont Theatre, where a reception was held in his honor and an orchestra played a selection of Boz waltzes that were composed specifically for the occasion! Just as music helped usher Dickens into the world the night before he was born, music again ushered him into the New World waiting for him in America.

*   *   *

The process had begun with this enormous amount of collective psychic energy being generated by the excitement of Charles Dickens's presence in America in *1842*. The question is, what happened to this energy? Energy can't be destroyed, but instead disperses, flowing in different directions until perhaps in a hundred years, it comes full circle, together again, and aims at its new target.

The scene in America changes to *1942* where, at the Paramount Theatre in New York, an unsuspecting young singer named Frank Sinatra is scheduled to do his very first solo performance. Before long, he would be the one pushing his way through a surging mob in the street, just like Dickens did. This time, however, press photographers would be on hand to photograph the event for posterity—the first clue, perhaps, that this young man might have something other to do, than to just sing.

*   *   *

Dickens, quickly tiring of all of the celebrating, soon got down to business. A journalist at heart, his social conscience was always foremost in what he set out to do. He had come to America, not to socialize, but to scale the social landscape by inspecting factory conditions, visiting poor houses, hospitals, prisons, lunatic and blind asylums. People were insulted when he began to turn down invitations to social events. They were likewise insulted when, later on, he avoided all mention in his travel book, *American Notes*, of the many celebrated receptions held in his honor that he attended while there. Even more offensive to the American psyche, was the fact that while Dickens wrote only brief descriptions of notable cities and critiques on various institutions, he wrote at length on an issue that no one wanted to hear about from a popular writer—slavery. Dickens didn't hesitate to speak out against this injustice while he was in America, and when the press started to attack him in the newspapers because of it, he became even more adamant and determined to speak his mind.

It has never been ascertained exactly why Charles Dickens was so intent on visiting America in the early days of his fame. The book he wrote from the information he gathered on his travels there was simply the means to pay for his expenses. Considering the long, uncomfortable and expensive journey, the compensation would hardly be adequate. The fact remains that Charles Dickens was not only intent on going to America; his unconscious motivation must have been exceptionally strong because he was practically obsessed with the idea!

In the light of the three chapters included in the book that deal specifically with pertinent issues: Chapter lll: *Boston*, Chapter Vll: *Philadelphia And Its Solitary Prison* and Chapter XVll: *Slavery*, it appears that certain destiny-making events were in the process of happening and that America, as a young, growing country, needed Charles Dickens and his phenomenal consciousness to help clear the way for progress.

BOSTON

In Boston, Dickens visited The Perkins Institute for the Blind, where he observed its founder Dr. Samuel Gridley Howe, and his helpers, working with blind children. The most notable of these children was Laura Bridgman, an eleven-year-old girl who was deaf, dumb, and blind, who had been brought there five years earlier, after Howe had found her living in a farmhouse in New Hampshire. Howe was immediately taken with the delicate but spirited Laura and persuaded the child's mother to entrust her to his care.

Dickens, too, was immediately captivated by the child from the moment he saw her. One of the girl's teachers, who was present on the day of his visit, recorded in her diary that "he did not deign to notice anything or anybody except Laura." It doesn't really matter what piqued his interest, what does matter is that he devoted so much space in his book, *American Notes*, to praising the Perkins School and the work it had done with Laura Bridgman.

Some forty years later, Helen Keller's mother would read *American Notes* and find hope and salvation in the book for her own deaf-blind daughter. She immediately contacted the Perkins school, where she found the perfect teacher for her child, Anne Sullivan. Helen Keller eventually became the living symbol for The American Foundation for the Blind when it was established, and she and her teacher became known the world over, in the words of Mark Twain, as "The Miracle and The Miracle Worker."

Few people have ever associated Charles Dickens with Helen Keller and The American Foundation for the Blind. To see the connection you must look under the surface of history and go back to the source, for this indeed is where the greatness of Charles Dickens lies, buried in the past, and for the most part, unrecognized today.

The pioneer work of Samuel Gridley Howe and his predecessors needed one thing—a spokesperson—and they couldn't have found a more effective one with a wider audience than Charles Dickens. The important role that he played did not end here, however; the author would continue to leave his mark when he returned to America twenty-five years later. In the interval, Howe had devised the first enduring system of Braille, The Boston Line Type, in the United States. One of the first novels to be printed in this form was *The Old Curiosity Shop* and Dickens himself paid the enormous expense of producing this embossed edition of his work while he was back in America in the sixties on his public reading tour.

*　*　*

Shortly after returning to England, Dickens encountered Samuel Gridley Howe in London at a benefit banquet for the Deaf and Dumb Provident Society, which Howe, along with his new wife, had come all the way from Boston to attend. At the dinner, Dickens was enormously amused to hear the young bride innocently address her husband as "darling", an endearment never used in public in polite Victorian society. Dickens, leaning back in his chair, jokingly inquired "Did she call him darling?" when his chair suddenly overturned and spilled him onto the floor, where he lay rolling about, doubled up with laughter.

It was Julia Ward Howe, who would go on to write *The Battle Hymn of the Republic* during the Civil War, who provoked the laughter that sent Charles Dickens rolling onto the floor at that dinner party. Interesting that he should be all dressed up in evening clothes for the occasion, and that music would in some way be associated with his achievement for the unseen minority, which would be of such vast importance for the plight of those condemned to a dungeon of darkness. The inspiration for this achievement was the enchanting and spirited Laura, whose laughter floated through the hallways, and whose familiar eyes and face Dickens had first seen in the misty light of the Perkins School for the Blind.

*　*　*

Had this event in Dickens's life somehow repeated itself in the next century, when Frank Sinatra was photographed for *Life* Magazine, dressed in evening clothes, rolling on the floor, doubled up with laughter, after his chair turned over at a dinner party? The issue of Life that this photograph appeared in was dated April of 1965, the hundredth anniversary of the Civil War ending.

This similar incident involving both Dickens and Sinatra brings attention to the fact that both men are indirectly linked to the Civil War exactly a hundred years apart. In the 1860's, Charles Dickens's books were a bright light in the darkness—one that had helped all of America through the Civil War—as his stories entertained soldiers at war, as well as a Nation at large.

In the 1960's, Frank Sinatra, whose voice had been a beacon of light for soldiers at war and the Nation at large twenty years before, was still a universal voice, speaking out for the continuing fight for rights that the Civil War had started the century before, and waging his own little war for the same cause on his home-turf in Las Vegas.

This connection could never have been made without a song, in this case the clue is "The Battle Hymn of the Republic", written for the Civil War by the woman who, in 1843, married Dr. Samuel Gridley Howe and became a surrogate mother for the fetching little deaf-blind girl named Laura.

A century later, Frank Sinatra would be the only one to sing the haunting song "Laura" and at the same time capture the mystery of the little deaf-blind girl with that name. Written in 1943, exactly one hundred years after Dickens had rolled on the floor in laughter at the benefit dinner for the Deaf and Dumb, the song enchanted Sinatra just as the girl Laura had enchanted Dickens. Voicing his preference for "Laura" as one of his favorite songs, Sinatra, later in life, requested the pianist, in the lounge of the Savoy Hotel In London, to play the song over and over again, without ever knowing what his unconscious motivation was to do so. He may possibly have been receiving some powerful vibes from the past by staying at a hotel located in Charles Dickens's London territory and by literally walking in his footsteps!

*   *   *

In June of 1962, while in Europe, Sinatra interrupted his "World Tour For The Children" in order to make a record album in London. *Frank Sinatra Sings Great Songs from Great Britain* is the only album that he ever recorded outside of the United States. A beautiful tribute to Britain and World War II, the album may also unconsciously be Sinatra's tribute to Charles Dickens and the myth that went before him.

There was a film made on this same visit to London called *Frank Sinatra And All God's Children*. Narrated by Sinatra, the film chronicles his visit to a school for the blind in London. Just as Dickens had come to

America and been captivated by a child at the Blind Asylum he visited, so would Frank Sinatra go to Britain and be captivated by the little children at The Sunshine House Nursery School for the Blind in London. The film doesn't lie; a beaming Frank Sinatra is seen walking hand in hand with, and amongst, the tiny inhabitants of the school, demonstrating once more that he was repeating a crucial experience from Dickens's life that had had far reaching consequence. It unquestionably makes sense to believe that, in our inheritance of instinct, this is an absolute prerequisite in order for one person to live another's myth.

PHILADELPHIA AND ITS SOLITARY PRISON

Charles Dickens's most famous visit to any Institution, anywhere, was probably his visit to the Eastern State Penitentiary in Philadelphia. Dickens, for the obvious reason that his father had at one time been incarcerated, was especially interested in penology and had visited prisons in Boston and New York. Neither visit had prepared him for the psychological horror that awaited his observation at this world-renown prison in Philadelphia. Built specifically for enforced solitary confinement, Eastern State was a model prison for the silent system of rehabilitation. Upon entering, the prisoner's clothes were taken from him, a dark hood was placed over his head and he was lead to his cell, never to emerge from it until his sentence was over. Having no contact with the outside world, and no communing within, prisoners would frequently go insane. Dickens immediately saw the inhumanness that the whole Pennsylvania Legislature had failed to foresee when they passed the bill to build the facility in the first place. Dickens's historic visit to this Penitentiary, and his stirring account of it, is considered to be the most powerful piece of writing in *American Notes*. Once again, his visit to an institution in America would have far reaching consequences. This time his words would aid all those who worked fervently for prison reform.

*   *   *

The following century, another aspect of the myth would be recorded on celluloid when Frank Sinatra was filmed, surrounded by prisoners, singing some *American notes* in a penitentiary! In this award-winning documentary on the singer's life and career, made for prime time television in 1965, the whole world had the opportunity to watch Sinatra doing the Dickens thing his way.

SLAVERY

Dickens, a resolute abolitionist, got his first look at slavery in Baltimore, Maryland, and was filled with shame and reproach when a slave waited on his dinner table. As he continued to travel as far south as Richmond, he was increasingly incensed by what he saw. The mere thought of being waited on by slaves filled him with dread and repugnance. It was impossible for him to keep silent on the subject while everyone expatiated on the virtues of slavery and expected him to agree! Not only did Dickens unreservedly speak his mind, but he also resolved that the world would hear how he felt about it. Nine years before *Uncle Tom's Cabin* was written, Charles Dickens addressed the subject of Slavery in America in a passionate chapter that he wrote for *American Notes*. He may very well have been the one to give Harriet Beecher Stowe the inspiration and the courage to write *Uncle Tom's Cabin,* the book that's been rumored to have helped start the Civil War.

In Washington, D.C., it was a slave who ushered Dickens in to meet the President of the United States. When Dickens was announced, President John Tyler expressed astonishment at seeing so young-looking a man. Dickens wished to return the compliment, but was unable to. The Chief Executive looked so old, worn and jaded that the words "you look well" stuck in Dickens's throat, and he was left speechless.

*   *   *

A little over a century later, in 1944, the youthful looking Frank Sinatra, still in the first flush of fame, also had an audience with the President of the United States. Accompanied by Rags Ragland and Toots

Shore, (two friends of his with names sounding right out of a Dickens novel), the intensely nervous Sinatra felt faint as he approached President Franklin Delano Roosevelt. The only words that the practically speechless Sinatra could muster up to greet the President with were Dickens's unspoken words "you look well".

The President returned the compliment by asking Sinatra where he acquired his hypnotic skills with the ladies? Sinatra told him, honestly, that he didn't know how he did it. No one had told him that Charles Dickens had mastered hypnosis, a hundred years before, by practicing the technique night and day on a lady (who incidentally wasn't his wife), while he was living in Genoa (the city of Sinatra's maternal roots) in 1844.

*　　*　　*

Dickens traveled as far south as Richmond, Virginia, and was so sickened by what he saw of slavery there, that he was forced to leave and turn back. At the very end of his long career, Frank Sinatra, who had been performing for almost sixty years, was also sickened and, for the first time, actually collapsed on stage in Richmond.

St. Louis was as far west as Dickens would travel on his first trip to America. On his second visit, twenty-five years later, ill health prevented him from going even as far as Chicago. At the time there was a great public outcry and general disappointment when his reading performances were canceled there.

A century later, Frank Sinatra may have been compensating for Dickens's slight on the city when he made two songs about Chicago famous. Taking the compensation a huge step further, Sinatra, later in life, packed up the band and made the long journey to Chicago by train, just as Dickens would have done at his age, in order to perform there. Leaving from the West Coast, Sinatra had to travel twice as far to reach Chicago, as Dickens would have from the East Coast, but paybacks—they say—are hell!

Sinatra, like Dickens, also left his mark in St. Louis. One of his most publicized performances was held there for the benefit of St.

Dismas House Orphanage. This time he brought The Rat Pack along and they were filmed while engaging in some modern day Pickwickian-type buffoonery.

*　　*　　*

There probably has never been a reception for any famous person, group, or dignitary, quite like the one that greeted Charles Dickens when he visited America in 1842. In Boston, they literally painted the whole town in preparation for his arrival. In New York, they celebrated with the incredibly sumptuous Boz Ball. In Philadelphia, a politician invited Dickens to meet a few of his friends in the lobby of his hotel, and he ended up shaking hands for two hours with hundreds of people. Everywhere Dickens went he was mauled, mobbed and lionized.

Blame it on his youth, (Dickens turned thirty while on this visit here), or the lack of privacy that left him little time or peace of mind to reflect on what he saw, Dickens's view of the country was limited. Being a highly intense person, he may have read too much into some things and exaggerated a bit. Dickens, however, wasn't one to suffer from tunnel vision. Neptunian in nature, he could see under the surface and get at the point of things. In striving to be honest and objective at the same time, most of what he had to say about America and its people, in his book *American Notes,* was fundamentally true.

At the time, America, as a new country, was overly sensitive. As a result, Americans were greatly offended. The truth hurts, but there is no growth without some discomfort. America needed to grow, for a century later, it would have to be ready to be number one.

5

From Here to Eternity

Exhausted from years of non-stop writing, Charles Dickens had taken off for America with his wife. After six months he returned, only to discover he was losing his popularity. While his *American Notes* caused a verbal uproar, his new novel *Martin Chuzzlewit* failed to rouse even a stir in England or elsewhere. For the first time, Dickens finds himself in financial straits. He changes publishers and is desperate for a comeback. Forced to summon up all of his creative powers, he changes his style, writing a Christmas story that spans *from here to eternity* and calls it *A Christmas Carol.* Dickens loses a lot of money on this book because he insisted it be elaborately bound. Intuitively, he knew the book's value, not only to himself, but also to posterity. The night he finished writing it, he threw down his pen, wept profusely, and ran outside where he walked alone up and down the dark streets of London all night long!

*   *   *

Exhausted from years of non-stop singing, Frank Sinatra divorces his wife, and takes off for Philadelphia to marry Ava Gardner. He, too, loses his popularity and finds himself in financial straits. Sinatra changes record labels, and is desperate for a comeback. He is forced to summon up all of his creative powers and changes his style. After reading the book *From Here to Eternity,* he fights for an acting role in the film that he intuitively knew would be perfect for him. Sinatra loses a lot of money acquiring the part, but wins an Academy Award for the performance. Later that same night, with his Oscar in hand, he walks alone up and down the dark streets of Beverly Hills all night long!

*   *   *

This brief period in *1844* was the only time in his long career that Charles Dickens's popularity was ever threatened, and the timing was incredibly bad. He still hadn't recovered financially from his trip to America the year before, and his wife had given birth to another child— a son they called Frank. Dickens was too distressed to even look at the new baby!

A hundred years later, in *1944,* a son, also called Frank, was born to Frank Sinatra and his wife. In the not too distant future, the marriage would fall apart and Sinatra would experience the only big threat to his career. Financially, the timing was incredibly bad for him also. When he is finally able to marry his Grand Passion, (Ava Gardner), he now can't afford to keep her!

*   *   *

With his expenses sky-high, his cash-flow poor, and his bank account overdrawn, Dickens, in an attempt to save money, rented out his big home in expensive London for a year, purchased a carriage and transported his family to Genoa, Italy, where it would be cheaper to live. It had to have been a huge carriage that took babies, nursemaids and other servants to Italy with Mr. and Mrs. Charles Dickens. It was a long hard trip, but Dickens was determined to make it. At the last minute, they even decided to bring the new baby, *Frank*, along with them to Genoa too.

Why Genoa? Again it appears as if some destiny-making events are in progress as Charles Dickens, just recently back from America, has the bug to leave England again, this time to go to live in the birthplace of Christopher Columbus, the man who discovered America in 1492. Dickens discovered America for himself in 1842, and who could anticipate what would happen in 1942? For now, Dickens's life mimicked a significant dream, which always reaches back to the past (Columbus) and at the same time, points ahead to the future (Sinatra).

Far away from the dirty, noisy streets of London, and from the spotlight of celebrity as well, Charles Dickens set down to write. He soon found out that he had failed to take one thing into consideration, and that was writer's block! The otherwise quiet streets of Genoa were alive with the sounds of church bells and they were driving him crazy. Inspiration came at last when Dickens decided to write his second Christmas story that turned into a nicely illustrated book with another musical title. He called the book *The Chimes*; the title inspired by the music from the church bells of Genoa.

* * *

Fifty years later, on a Christmas day in this very same town in Italy, a baby girl named Natalie *Catherine* was born to a family of educated lithographers, with a musical background, who were, no doubt, also inspired by the church bells of Genoa. This little girl they called *Dolly* lived in Genoa two years before coming to America and one day becoming the mother of Frank Sinatra.

* * *

One can only imagine how the Genoese took to having a person of the celebrity of Charles Dickens living amongst them. For almost a decade, people had gathered in groups, in towns and villages, to have the monthly installments of his current novel read to them. Illiterate people would sometimes only know it was the first day of the month because this was the day Dickens's monthly serial arrived. Considering that most of the people living then didn't know how to read, that there was no radio or television, and that even live entertainment was limited, gives some idea of just how popular a celebrity Charles Dickens really was there.

The lively thirty-two year old author, still in his youthful prime, and his lovely English wife, *Catherine*, must have been just as captivating to the Genoese, as the characters in his novels had been in the seven years preceding their arrival there.

*   *   *

Taking a look at Frank Sinatra's celebrated life, one can get a pretty good idea of the influence that Dickens had in nineteen-century Italy when it came to naming the future generation of children. Sinatra's grandmother Rose, his mother Dolly, his father Martin Anthony, and his first wife, Nancy Rose, may all have been named after the famed characters in Dickens's wildly popular early novels *Oliver Twist, Barnaby Rudge,* and *Martin Chuzzlewit.*

After Dickens left Genoa and wrote *David Copperfield,* the influence again becomes apparent when, in the book, Dickens describes the youthful passion and romance of David with his sweetheart *Dora* and their subsequent wedding, which is the most celebrated event of its type in all of Dickens's novels.

In the twentieth century, magazines everywhere carried an early photograph of Frank Sinatra, as a tiny boy, dressed in a tux for his Aunt Dora's wedding. Frank Sinatra's life, at the early age of three, was also mimicking a significant dream by reaching back to the past with the name *Dora* and, at the same time, pointing ahead to the future with a tuxedo!

*   *   *

Charles Dickens loved the friendliness and warmth of the Italian people he met everywhere he traveled in Italy, but living in Genoa for a whole year left a distinct impression of the Genoese that he passed on in a letter he wrote to his best friend John Forster, in which he enlightens us as to the probable reason why Frank Sinatra had a tendency to throw punches. In the letter, Dickens, sounding perfectly *frank*, describes the Genoese manner as "exceedingly animated and pantomimic; so that two friends of the lower class conversing pleasantly in the street, always seem on the eve of stabbing each other forthwith. And a stranger is immensely astonished at their not doing it."

*   *   *

The restless Dickens wasn't content to stay put in Italy and the moment he finished writing *The Chimes*, he was out of there! Braving bad weather and hazardous traveling conditions, the author made his way back to London in time to deliver the completed manuscript, oversee illustrations and even do a preview reading of his little Christmas book to a small group of literary friends at John Forster's home in Lincoln Inn Fields. Among those present was the great Shakespearean actor, William Charles Macready, and he along with everyone else was reduced to tears at Dickens's emotional presentation. Talk of the dramatic reading spread throughout London, heralding the fact that the evening had been a total triumph for Dickens. This was definitely *the start of something great*, for with this smash presentation, Dickens unconsciously began preparing for his later performing career as a public reader.

Braving the miles and the elements again, the author arrived back in Italy in time to spend Christmas day with his wife Catherine and their children. With the publication of his second little Christmas book, *The Chimes*, Charles Dickens's name became synonymous with Christmas and remains so to this very day.

*   *   *

Dickens would go on to write three more Christmas books after *The Chimes*. None, however, would compare to *A Christmas Carol*. While Carol had failed to extricate Dickens from the financial bind that he was in at the time, there is no disputing that it performed a service of longer lasting value for its author. With the story that spanned *from here to eternity*, Dickens made his comeback and would never have to worry about money or waning popularity again for the rest of his life.

Writing in a letter that he was "as brown as a berry" from basking in the Italian sunshine, Dickens, feeling peaceful and rested, left Italy and returned to London, settling back in Devonshire Terrace with his family. He could now pick up where he left off before he went to America, as the undisputed king of the novel. No longer would he have to worry about supporting his growing family and he could even look fondly on his baby, Frank, who he had affectionately nicknamed "Chickenstalker" while they were living in Genoa.

* * *

Frank Sinatra also wrote in a letter addressed to his daughter Nancy, who he affectionately called "Chicken," that he was "as brown as a berry." Many years had gone by since the film *From Here to Eternity* had performed a service of lasting value for him, as *A Christmas Carol* had done for Dickens, and *from this moment on*, the singer would also never have to worry about money or waning popularity ever again.

6

BAUBLES, BANGLES AND BEADS

Returning to London after a year in Italy, a new challenge awaited Charles Dickens when he became editor of The Daily News. Dickens edited the newspaper for only a short time, but gained the valuable experience he would need later to edit the two remarkably innovative successful weekly magazines that he eventually founded. These magazines were vehicles of communication for Dickens, enabling him to address all of his social concerns, while at the same time providing entertainment and other news to his readers. This endeavor also allowed Dickens complete control over the publications, as well as the opportunity to prove himself the greatest magazine editor of all time!

As remarkable as the tremendous fame he had achieved as an author was, as well as his growing fame as an actor, Dickens would now become famous as a conductor of weeklies. In this capacity, it was almost as though Dickens were conducting an orchestra while his collaborators were always on standby with their instruments, in this case, their pens. The versatile Dickens would always be sure to have a hand in everything: he would edit the magazine, be the lead writer and guide the other writers, review books and answer queries. It's not difficult to conjure up a picture in one's mind of Dickens at work, a cigarette in hand, waving his arm and ordering his staff to "brighten it, brighten it!"

All of this was going on in the round building by the Strand, in the city of London, where his office was located. One even has to wonder if, all of the while, Dickens wasn't wearing a hat!

*　　*　　*

It's even easier to conjure up a picture of Frank Sinatra, at the same age as Dickens, a cigarette in hand, wearing a hat and working in the round building in the city of the angels, basically doing with music all that Charles Dickens was doing with prose: choosing songs carefully, helping to lie out arrangements, weaving a spell with the lyrics, sometimes waving his arm conducting the orchestra and perhaps even ordering the musicians to "brighten it!" The singer even went so far as to produce an album called *Tone Poems in Color* on which he personally conducted the orchestra! Becoming increasingly visible for his versatility as an artist, like Charles Dickens before him, Frank Sinatra had to have a hand in every stage of the production.

*　　*　　*

To Dickens's vast amusement, his office boy William Edrupt was not one of his fans. Every once in a while he would ask the boy if he had read any of his books yet and when Edrupt replied "no sir", Dickens would reward him with a hearty slap on the back and the response "good boy!"

Working in the gambling pits in Las Vegas in the 1960's was a young Pit boss by the name of Ed Walters who, no matter how hard he tried, Sinatra was unable to interest in listening to his music. Sinatra even offered to fly Ed out to Los Angeles to attend one of his recording sessions but Ed declined. He asked Sinatra why he should go all the way to LA to hear him sing, when he had to listen to him singing while he was working!

*　　*　　*

Shortly after resigning as editor of The Daily News, Dickens felt the need to involve himself in some new philanthropic endeavors. He took an interest in prostitutes and with the financial help of banking heiress, Angela Burdett-Coutts, he set up a home for reforming them, taking an active part in not only running the establishment, but in counseling the young women as well.

Dickens also set up The Guild of Literature and Art, initially a relief fund for retired writers in need. Later, support was extended to struggling artists. Dickens was influential in persuading his colleague, Sir Edward Bulwar-Lytton, to donate land on his estate, Knebworth, for new accommodations to be built on, as a place of refuge for impoverished writers to live. Although enough money was raised to complete the project, their efforts were wasted. No writers or artists ever came to live there, as many of them were just too proud to do so.

*　　*　　*

While Frank Sinatra would repeat this philanthropic pattern, he was able to avoid Dickens's misjudgments. Sinatra can be seen on film, being interviewed by Edward R. Murrow, explaining the relief fund he had set up for retired actors, and accommodations weren't mentioned. As to Sinatra's relationship with prostitutes, he also supported them, except in another capacity! Had he, indeed, learned something from Dickens's somewhat wasted efforts?

*　　*　　*

It's possible that Charles Dickens may have become more broad-minded on the subject of prostitutes when, in middle age, permanently separated from his wife, he frequented Paris with his younger friends,

Wilkie Collins and Augustus Egg, where he smoked, drank and supposedly had his first encounter with a prostitute. Is there any question why (oh, why!) Dickens would proclaim, "*I love Paris?*"

And, once more, it's easy to conjure-up a picture of the middle aged Frank Sinatra in Paris, especially if you've seen him in the 1960 film, *Can-Can,* still slim and dressed in similar period clothing as Charles Dickens in Paris in 1860! Hollywood's own myth-making once more seems to be recording aspects of the real myth on celluloid.

* * *

An additional challenge awaited Charles Dickens on his return from Italy, and this was the pressing need to reinvent himself after the disappointing sales of his latest novel, *Martin Chuzzelwit.* As before, he packed up his family but this time they went to live in Switzerland for a year. Once settled, Dickens begins writing the first of his series of dark novels, *Dombey and Son,* in which he incorporates symbolism, for the first time, as a form of social analysis.

The author was probably unaware that he was on the threshold of discovering a new literary sphere because, after completing the dark Dombey, he reverted to his lighter style again, writing *David Copperfield,* one of the most popular novels of all time. Copperfield, considered to be largely autobiographical, was a therapeutic vehicle for Dickens. Although the author was not yet in the *September of his years,* he had begun to look back at his life and analyze it.

It was in the 1850's, with Copperfield behind him, that Charles Dickens would experience tremendous growth in his art. The author, perplexing critics and readers alike, proceeded to produce a string of profoundly symbolic masterpieces; each novel incorporating some form of social analysis. Dickens had never lost sight of his goal of heightening awareness in his readers in an attempt to help a changing society understand the many problems that endangered it. The quandary was that Dickens was so far ahead of his time (surpassing even Freud by delving into depth psychology and symbolism years before Carl Jung was even born), that the genius of his later novels went largely unrecognized for more than a half century.

*   *   *

It was also in the fifties, a century later, that Frank Sinatra would produce a series of dark masterpieces on the Capitol label that would benefit the progression of self-analysis and help a changing society understand the many new psychological problems that endangered it.

The effect Sinatra's torch albums had on the collective psyche is still not generally understood, but there is not much doubt that they were, and still are, conducive to self-reflection, which is the crucial ingredient in the process of psychic growth. Incredibly, Frank Sinatra, who is said to have invented *depth* in singing, had been doing this from the beginning, as his was the voice, even then full of feeling and expression, that cried out in the wasteland of the war years and comforted people.

*   *   *

Restless and unfulfilled in his marital relationship, Dickens would throw himself wholeheartedly into amateur theatricals as a diversion. He would produce, direct, star in and sometimes even write the script for the show, the proceeds from which benefited various charities and institutions. He'd often take his show on the road, performing in the provinces throughout Great Britain and achieving widespread fame as a talented actor.

Unexpectedly, in his mid-forties, Charles Dickens fell in love with a fair-haired, eighteen-year old actress named Ellen Ternan, who was appearing in one of his plays. The two actually met on the stage set. Dickens, who had two daughters around the same age as the young actress, had little hope of establishing a romantic relationship with Ellen but came to love her passionately all the same. The focusing of these intense feelings on his beloved left Dickens no recourse but to finally face the music: he and his wife had long been incompatible, and he was hopelessly trapped and unhappy. Divorce wasn't an option for most people in the nineteenth century, but for Charles Dickens, a public figure who symbolized domestic harmony and Christian virtue, it was impossible!

Dickens loved Ellen Ternan secretly and tragically for the rest of his life. When he died, he confounded everyone by mentioning her name first in his will. It was the only way that he could finally tell the whole world that he had loved her.

∗   ∗   ∗

Restless and unhappy from the break-up of his marriage to Ava Gardner, Frank Sinatra would also throw himself wholeheartedly into performing on stage with the modern day Pickwickian type buffoons famed as The Rat Pack. Like Dickens, he also took the show on the road at times, doing benefit performances for various charities and institutions.

In his mid-forties, Frank Sinatra also unexpectedly fell in love with a fair-haired young actress, still in her teens, by the name of Mia Farrow, who he met on a stage set as well. Sinatra, who also had two daughters around the same age as Mia, initially had little intention of establishing a serious romantic relationship with her but it happened nevertheless. Sinatra proposed marriage to Mia while he was in *London* making a film, but married her in the States. The couple went directly back to *London* for their *honeymoon*, before purchasing and settling in an *English Tudor Mansion* in Beverly Hills. It remained a mystery to Sinatra and everyone else as to why he went so far as to marry Mia Farrow in the first place. Years later, speaking about the marriage to journalist Pete Hamill, Sinatra remarked, "I still don't know what that was all about!"

Was Frank Sinatra resolving some more of Dickens's karma and was he in some way compensating for Dickens (who was not able to marry Ellen Ternan) when he married Mia Farrow? Mia took a fancy to calling Sinatra "*Charlie*" and even purchased *London cab* for him as a birthday gift. Although the marriage lasted only a year and a half, Mia Farrow's "doll face" (as Sinatra called her) with the large caption "Mrs.

Sinatra", graced the cover of *Life* Magazine for all the world to see. Dickens, for one, would have been the most pleased to see it!

* * *

Ultimately, it was the long build-up of unconscious suppression that propelled the unexpected to happen in Dickens's life; and relief came in a way never dreamed of. *A bracelet* he bought for the actress *Ellen Ternan,* which got into his wife's hands, finally triggered the end of Dickens's marriage. When the jeweler delivered the bracelet to Dickens's house by mistake, a horrible blow-up ensued when his wife realized it was not for her, and their separation followed.

A bracelet he bought for actress *Lana Turner,* that got into first wife Nancy's hands, also triggered the end of Sinatra's first marriage. Mistakenly thinking it was for her, a horrible blow-up ensued when his wife realized it was not, and their separation followed.

Bracelets for *Ellen Ternan* and *Lana Turner?*
"Baubles, Bangles and Beads," indeed!

7

THE MIRACLE OF THE BELLS

Initially, few people realized that Charles Dickens and his wife Catherine had separated, and no one anticipated the scandal that would follow after his in-laws began spreading rumors that Dickens was involved with a young actress. While he was emotionally attached to actress Ellen Ternan, it's doubtful that he was actually involved with her sexually as yet. Dickens, who had an image to uphold and whose very name was associated with a happy home, seethed with anger. With a large family to support, he feared the rumors could adversely impair his earning power.

As the horrible scandal spread, Dickens became delusional in thinking that by now the whole world must know. Hastily, he issued a statement on his long-standing domestic trouble, which appeared on the front page of his monthly magazine, as well as in many newspapers, sparking curiosity in readers who knew nothing about it.

More determined than ever to handle this his way, he ended up making matters worse by writing an even more explicit letter to be used exclusively by his manager to show in his defense to anyone who had been misled into believing lies spoken about him. Unfortunately, the letter fell into the hands of a newspaperman who published it in the New York Tribune, from which the newspapers in Britain later copied it. Dickens had not authorized publication of what he came to call the "violated letter"; he had wrongly and naively assumed that it would be kept a "private and personal communication".

The scandal now spread rapidly, as the anguished Dickens stood by watching and not being able to control what was happening. The irony of the situation was that, in the end, the needless publicity of this detestable scandal finally gave Charles Dickens his freedom, but not without the cost of tremendous suffering and emotional turmoil. The greater tragedy was that, because of the age that he lived in, Dickens was never able to divorce his wife legally. Instead he divorced her in the true sense of the word, with his unyielding determination to never lay eyes on her again.

*   *   *

It would take another hundred years for the first big tabloid love scandal to become breaking news in the media. Precisely at mid-century, the scandal broke involving Frank Sinatra and the beautiful movie actress, Ava Gardner. Sinatra, like Dickens, had a "happy home" image to uphold and people were shocked when he left his wife and children to go off with the sultry screen star. Sinatra, determined to do it his way, was able to divorce his first wife and marry Ava Gardner, but only at the same cost of tremendous suffering and emotional turmoil as Dickens.

*   *   *

Financially, Charles Dickens and Frank Sinatra both supported their ex-wives handsomely for the rest of their lives. Dickens supported so many others, besides those close to him, that his financially lucrative public reading performances became a necessity.

His relationship with actress Ellen Ternan, and the help of her theatrical family, enabled Dickens to become a masterful performer. The effect of Ellen Ternan's presence, while he was performing, gave Dickens confidence and helped him establish a good rapport with his audience. Two months before Dickens retired, Ellen was in attendance at a special reading he gave before professional actors. Dickens's performance was so absolutely electrifying on this occasion that many people began to wonder if he had a professional reading coach. Dickens consciously suppressed any suggestion that he received coaching from anyone, let alone Ellen Ternan, because he had to protect her reputation as well as his own. Arousing even more suspicion was the fact that Dickens had adapted *the relaxed, effortless and natural style of acting* that was characteristic of the Ternan family.

∗　　∗　　∗

Sinatra also supported many people besides those close to him. It was his relationship with Ava Gardner, and the deep feelings it evoked, that also enabled him to become a masterful performer. Listening to Sinatra sing pre-Ava on Columbia, there is a world of difference from listening to him sing post-Ava on Capitol. All it took was *one touch of Venus!*

Sinatra also denied that he had had a vocal coach, but again it wasn't true. The month or so that he spent with one, in the beginning of his career, taught him the basics, but it was Ava Gardner who taught Frank Sinatra how to reach into his soul and really sing the blues! Long after they divorced, Sinatra followed Ava around the world, arranging performances so that she could be in attendance. Gone were the days when Ava would storm out of the room in a jealous rage if Sinatra sang about Nancy, nearly as upset as Ellen Ternan must have been when Dickens, to the detriment of his health, read about Nancy!

Eventually, Frank Sinatra came to adapt the same *relaxed, effortless and natural style of performing* that was characteristic of Charles Dickens.

Sinatra would take the art a step further, employing his acting voice while he was singing the lyrics to songs.

*   *   *

Charles Dickens's live performances were to the nineteenth century, what Frank Sinatra's live performances were to the twentieth. They were *The Main Event!* Exuberant shouts of "Dickens is coming" echoed in towns where he was announced to read. His arrival on a train platform was greeted with cheers that could be heard a block away, and nothing would deter people from standing outside all night long waiting to purchase tickets the next morning.

Dickens performed to audiences of boisterous men who once even stormed the stage, picked him up and tried to carry him away! The author had been evoking emotional response in the minds and hearts of his readers for twenty years before he ever stepped foot on stage to present his writings in this unique form of entertainment. Dickens's performances were not literal readings; they were a one-man show in which Dickens would bring a host of his characters to life with his spectacular acting skills, employing an astonishing conveyance of body language and vocalism at the same time.

After ten years of continued success performing almost exclusively in Britain, Dickens began to seriously consider some of the more lucrative offers he had received from other countries as far away as Australia. He opted to go to Australia initially, as two of his sons were then living there, but changed his mind as he began to feel himself drawn once more towards America, as fatefully as Darnay (in *A Tale of Two Cities)* had been drawn to the Loadstone Rock in Paris.

When it was announced in the sixties that Charles Dickens was returning to America after a twenty-four year interval, the press called it "The Second Coming." His six-month reading tour was advertised on bright orange-colored posters that appeared everywhere. Orange was Charles Dickens's favorite color. All of his books, beginning with Pickwick, had been advertised on orange paper, and so were all of his reading performances. Orange, the color of geraniums, (the flower that Dickens always wore in his lapel while he was performing), had attended Charles Dickens on the road to wealth and fame. Orange was his lucky color and it is no wonder that he was partial to it!

*   *   *

It was in the sixties of the following century that America discovered that orange was also Frank Sinatra's favorite color. For over twenty-five years now, Sinatra had evoked an emotional response in the minds and hearts of his listeners, and in April of 1965, when *Life* Magazine featured a picture of him on the cover clad in an orange sweater, his fans got to learn something entirely new about him. *Look* Magazine quickly followed suit in December with a cover story on *Sinatra at Fifty*. Dressed in orange, the singer is seen standing in the predominately orange-colored decor of his Palm Springs home. Sinatra often wore an orange handkerchief in the breast pocket of his jacket while he was performing and would pull one out occasionally to give to one of his fans in the audience as a souvenir.

It seems pretty obvious now that, in their hearts, both Charles Dickens and Frank Sinatra belonged to *tangerine*!

*   *   *

It was still *autumn in New York* when Dickens arrived there in 1867 on his second visit to America, only to find himself as well known, and as recognizable, as he was in London. On Broadway, every window seemed to have his picture on display, and every theater marquee to feature the title of one of his works. Dickens stayed at the Westminster Hotel in Irving Place where a guard was assigned to be in constant attendance outside his sitting room. He was able to come and go, unseen by the public, via a private stairway that he would have exclusive use of.

Meanwhile, pandemonium was taking place in front of Steinway Hall, where his readings were being held, with over 5,000 people standing in line for a chance to purchase tickets for one of his shows. It was his manager Dolby's dilemma that he couldn't fit all 5,000 people into a hall that held only 2,000, and thousands unhappily had to be turned away.

Not even the early snowfall of eighteen inches or bitterly cold weather would stop people from standing in line all night long, as bonfires blazed and riots broke out among the disappointed speculators. With this storm, severe weather set in for practically the duration of the tour, and making matters worse, Charles Dickens had a cold that would last even longer. By the time of the first performance, every four-wheeled vehicle in the entire city had been altered and made into a sleigh. It must have been quite a sight to see Central Park abuzz with what seemed to be thousands of sleighs, as well as the scores of people dressed in their Victorian garb arriving in them, at Steinway Hall, in the snow-covered streets of nineteenth-century New York. Magic was definitely abroad in the frosty air because Charles Dickens was performing there!

*　　*　　*

Dickens rode the rails between Boston and New York in December of that year, varying reading performances for the holiday season. There must have been as few people alive then, as there are today, who would not want to have been present among the awe struck audience, at the Tremont Temple in Boston, who witnessed Charles Dickens himself reading *A Christmas Carol* on Christmas Eve in 1867.

In January, Dickens headed south to his first stop in Philadelphia, performing in the Concert Hall on Chestnut Street that, fifty years later, would become the first Roseland Ballroom. (It would move to New York after one year because of the restrictive Pennsylvania Blue Laws). The author was holed up two blocks away at *The Continental*; the daring, immense hotel that sat on the very same spot at 9th and Chestnut Streets were the old Benjamin Franklin Hotel still stands today. (It was in the Garden Terrace Room at the Benjamin Franklin that Harry James debuted his Orchestra in 1939 in a prelude to his discovering Frank Sinatra.)

Continuing his journey south, Dickens read in Baltimore, a city that he felt was still haunted by the ghost of slavery. Practically on the eve of the impeachment of President Andrew Johnson, he was performing in Washington, D.C., choosing to ignore The New York Tribune editor's warning to avoid the city because the rowdy element was in full force there. Despite this, Dickens's first Washington reading turned out to be a brilliant occasion with the President, his Cabinet, the Supreme Court and every Ambassador in attendance. (The pattern of this brilliant occasion would repeat itself more than once when, in the next century, Frank Sinatra performed in Washington, D.C. for more than one President).

On February 7, 1868, Dickens celebrated his fifty-sixth birthday in Washington, D.C. by visiting the White House, where he had an audience with President Johnson. On returning to his hotel, he found his sitting room filled with flowers, congratulatory cards, letters, telegrams and presents delivered from all over the country. All of America, it seemed, had remembered his birthday!

Valentine's Day appropriately found Dickens back in Philadelphia, the City of Brotherly Love, giving a farewell reading performance there. His cold persisted and in March he was forced to cancel his shows in Chicago because he wasn't up to traveling a thousand miles by train. Publisher George W. Childs, of the Philadelphia Public Ledger, advised him "if you don't read in Chicago the people will go into fits". Dickens replied "Well, I would rather they went into fits than I did!"

(Almost like an afterthought, later in life, Frank Sinatra and his band made that Chicago trip down the long *lonesome road* by train to perform there, decades after air travel had become the predominate means of traveling long distances).

With spring approaching, Dickens was able to fit in reading performances in Syracuse, Buffalo and Rochester, New York. It almost seems myth-mandatory that Charles Dickens, who left us a picture of the nineteenth century in a rich legacy of words, and who considered Rochester, England his hometown, would make his way into its namesake Rochester, New York, the city that would become the home of pictures-on-film in the twentieth century.

*　　*　　*

Having come full circle from his first visit here, twenty-five years earlier, Charles Dickens prepared to leave America with a final farewell reading in New York, quoting from his autobiographical novel, *David Copperfield*, the words "my future life lies over the sea." The paradox is that he wrote these words in England, and he uttered them in New York, giving the words a double meaning. In America, the brief remainder of his mortal life did lie over the sea in England, just as he said. But who can say that the same words, when he wrote them in England, didn't unconsciously mean that in another lifetime, in another century, he'd be living somewhere *beyond the sea* in America?

The audience listened in rapt silence as Charles Dickens ended his farewell speech with "God bless you, and God bless the land in which I leave you". The following day, crowds of people gathered in the street in front of the Westminster Hotel, cheering and throwing flowers down from the windows on to Charles Dickens as he left New York for the last time. He had brought something precious (his own presence) to America and now he was leaving something precious behind (the memory of that presence).

*   *   *

The scene in America changes drastically by the year of 1942. New York City is busier than ever and cars and buses have replaced the horse and carriage. There are still many theater marquees, but now they are all lit up with electric lights. One marquee stands out because it not only has words written on it, but also displays a huge image of the face of a young man, with luminous eyes not unlike those of Charles Dickens. His name is Frank Sinatra, and once again, there are long lines of people waiting in line all night long to buy tickets to see one man perform.

But this time around, all five thousand (the number of people who had waited in line to get in to see Dickens) people would be accommodated at the Paramount Theater and in their places when the unprepared Jack Benny introduced a singer he had never heard of by the name of Frank Sinatra. Benny had the surprise of his life when a mad rush up to the stage, of screaming fans, nearly knocked him off the ramp as he was exiting the stage Sinatra had just walked out onto. Unsuspectingly, Sinatra stepped out on to the stage, and when he opened his mouth to sing, an unearthly howl arose from the audience. The balconies began to shake with the uproar and the management of the theater began to panic. Sinatra, intensely frightened, could barely get the words out to the opening song. As a diversion, the band was immediately ordered to start playing *The National Anthem* and, for the moment, Frank Sinatra's opening song had to wait until the commotion, which seemingly had come from nowhere, died down.

The commotion, however, may very possibly have come from somewhere. It takes a lot of energy to fire up such sudden collective hysteria. As mentioned before, that energy may have been generated a hundred years earlier, in 1842, by the shared excitement caused by Charles Dickens's first visit here. Having dispersed, this accumulated energy had now come back around in the spiral of time, growing into a tightly wound cyclone which, like a huge gust of wind that had somehow made its way into the Paramount and become trapped, formed a ball and moved at hurricane speed, as it readied itself to infuse its new target—Frank Sinatra!

It was a charmed moment in time. Years later Sinatra recalled his one big moment by describing the sound as "absolutely deafening; a tremendous roar of thousands, stamping, yelling, screaming and applauding", until it seemed "the roof would come off." The event is still remembered but the song chosen to launch the single longest most fabulous career of the century is all but forgotten. The truth is that when the intensely frightened Sinatra opened his mouth to sing, the words "*the bells are ringing*" just wouldn't come out!

"*Ring-a-ding ding!!*" Only in America could this happen. America—whose myth had begun with the birth of Christopher Columbus in the city of Genoa where the bells are ringing perpetually. Who would have thought in the panic of that day just how appropriate it was to substitute the words "*the bells are ringing*" with the music of the National Anthem. It was truly *the miracle of the bells*!

Many years later, looking back on his early fame, Frank Sinatra would ponder: "Sometimes I wonder whether anybody ever had it like I had it, before or since. It was the darndest thing, wasn't it?" Charles Dickens, knowingly, would have agreed.

8

LONDON BY NIGHT

I t seems that every time something truly significant happens in one's life, you can usually look back about two years and see what was unnoticed by you at the time; that fate was busily preparing for the significant event to occur. So it was that Charles Dickens, a couple of years prior to his separation from his wife, would realize a childhood dream by purchasing a house in the country, which he had long set his heart on owning. Located southeast of London, near Rochester, this modest brick house is situated on a historic spot called Gad's Hill, where Shakespeare wrote of Falstaff robbing the travelers in *Henry V*. The highlight of the property is its secluded ambience, set as it is in the beautiful wooded countryside surrounding the house. This home afforded Dickens the privacy he would need to escape the spotlight of celebrity and the pressures of living in the big city. Since he would soon be approaching the biggest scandal of his life after separating from his wife and entering into a secret liaison with actress Ellen Ternan, the privacy of Gad's Hill would come in handy!

Ironically preceding the end of Dickens's marriage came a change in the pattern of his life and friendships, as many of his old companions from earlier days had died. He now surrounded himself almost exclusively with younger men who were literary contemporaries. *Young at heart*, the restless Dickens could still party with the best of them! But, despite his nocturnal escapades, in the company of the likes of novelist Wilkie Collins in the green rooms of London and Paris, Dickens yearned for the romantic ideal of love and domestic serenity.

Desperately unhappy and obsessed with breaking ties with his past, Dickens disposed of his large house in London and made Gad's Hill his home base for the rest of his life. Spending a large part of his free time there, he gradually transformed it into a small estate, adding on to the house and erecting other structures on the property, which included having a *Swiss chalet* built in the wooded area. With its spacious lawn and *circular driveway in the front* of the house, and meadowlands in the back, Dickens could enjoy the vista while listening to the wrens and larks singing by day and the nightingales by night. He worked diligently to enhance the homey comforts of Gad's Hill and was extremely proud of his accomplishment.

The house was frequently filled with guests and the overflow would be put up at the Inn across the road. Dickens would personally see to it that each room was equipped with every comfort. There would always be an easy chair included with the bedroom furniture, a fully equipped desk, a small library of books, a side table with teapot and accessories and, in cooler weather, a roaring fire in the fireplace of each room.

Every guest at Gad's Hill could do as they pleased and feel right at home on the premises. Breakfast was served at nine and lunch at one, at which time the dinner menu would be displayed on the sideboard for inspection. Dickens, who wrote all morning, emerged at lunchtime and anyone who wished to join him on his daily walk along the quiet country lanes was invited to do so. Upon returning from his walk, he'd immediately begin organizing outdoor games, which he would then participate in with more zest than anyone!

The highlight of the day for the guests, however, was dining with their illustrious host. The delight he felt in companionship showed in Charles Dickens's glowing face and bright eyes. He was an excellent listener who spoke little of himself and always brought out the best in others. The times when he did speak, he was so comical that he often had to refrain from laughing at himself. After dinner, the guests would be entertained with music, dancing and games; charades, memory games and pantomimes were his favorites. Late in the evening, after the ladies retired, the men had their whiskey and smoked in the billiard room, often not retiring until dawn set in.

Dickens, who spent most of his time on trains traveling between towns while he was performing, would retreat to Gad's Hill in between tours to rest and recuperate. He loved animals and surrounded himself with pet birds, cats, and dogs, and was often seen walking one of his dogs along the country roads. He had successfully created an environment that he and his children could call "home" and, at the same time, a place where he could entertain the people he was most fond of. There was never a host quite like Charles Dickens; that is, not until Frank Sinatra, who repeated this pattern of hospitality at his estate in Palm Springs.

*   *   *

Fate had also been preparing for a significant event to happen in Frank Sinatra's life when it took him to Palm Springs, California, in the late forties. Sinatra was also approaching the biggest scandal of his life when, separating from his wife, he entered into a liaison with actress Ava Gardner. He too would need the privacy the remote location of the desert area afforded as an escape from the spotlight of celebrity and the pressures of living in the big city.

With so much of his free time spent at Palm Springs, Sinatra eventually purchased a modest house with secluded grounds and transformed it into a small estate, adding on to the house and erecting other structures on the property, which included a cottage he called *The Christmas Tree House*. With its spacious lawn and *circular driveway in the front*, and the desert view in the back, Sinatra had also worked diligently to enhance the homey comforts of his Palm Springs home and was proud of his accomplishment.

The Compound, as he called it, was frequently filled with guests and Sinatra would personally see to it that each room was equipped with every comfort. The kitchen staff was available around the clock, ready to prepare any type food or drink requested. Every guest at Palm Springs could do as they pleased and feel at home; the highlight of the day being the evening spent with their illustrious host. Sinatra delighted in companionship, spoke little of himself and brought out the best in others. He was never short on ideas of how to keep his guests pleasantly occupied, and that often included playing charades!

After dinner the ladies retreated to a room to chat and have coffee while the men smoked and drank Jack Daniels whiskey in another room. Being the twentieth century, guests would then file into the movie room, where a newly released film was shown. Sinatra, however, rarely joined them for the movie but retreated instead to another building on the premises that had been built specifically to house his million-dollar train collection. While his guests watched the movie, Sinatra would be deep in thought watching the miniature train for hours as it moved along the tracks, as though some vague memory from the nineteenth century was beckoning him back there!

Just as Charles Dickens had done, Frank Sinatra had created an environment for himself in Palm Springs that he and his children could call "home" and, at the same time, a place where he could entertain the people he was most fond of. Sinatra would retreat there from the weariness of performing life. He loved animals and surrounded himself with pet birds and dogs and was often seen walking one of his dogs along the desert lanes.

The house in Palm Springs with its Christmas Tree House (or Swiss Chalet, call it what you like), the orange walls, orange rugs and orange furniture may have been telling us something about Frank Sinatra that no one could hear until now.

*   *   *

Part of the appeal for Charles Dickens of having a country estate like Gad's Hill was that it was within reasonable distance for traveling to the city. Wherever the cosmopolitan Dickens lived, whether it be Gad's Hill or abroad in Italy, France or Switzerland, he would always long for London, the city he called his "magic lantern". He claimed the maze of streets and the crowds rushing through the thoroughfares supplied the stimulation to his brain that was absolutely necessary for him to write. When he would experience writer's block, it took just one visit to London to set him up and get him to start all over again.

A foggy day in London would find Dickens conducting business there, but it was the wonderful sight of *London by night* that, from the time he was a child, had never failed to excite and stimulate him. Only at night would London appear unchanged as the place where the boy Dickens became a man. It was on its streets that he had educated himself and it was the one place he could always depend on to go home to. It wasn't unusual for him to walk the streets of London all night until dawn, stopping at coffee houses and his other favorite haunts. It was his night expeditions to the darker side of London, and the people that frequented these areas, that would provide him with information he would use for his books. A regular stop for Dickens was the station house where he would talk with police inspectors and detectives, and be escorted by them as he walked among the poor while observing derelicts, criminals and the dying. Dickens's later novels reflect his fascination for police work and detectives. His last novel, the unfinished masterpiece, *The Mystery of Edwin Drood*, is the first great mystery novel to feature not only a *detective*, but also *a musician with a beautiful voice,* as it's main character.

*   *   *

The cosmopolitan Frank Sinatra had all the great cities of the world at his disposal but it was to the night magic of New York City that he always had the urge to return to. In the shadowy regions of the city he would visit his favorite haunts and not leave until dawn. This was the place where the boy Sinatra became a man, on whose streets he had educated himself, and that he could always depend on to go home to.

Frank Sinatra obviously also had a fascination for police work and detectives, which is apparent from the films, incorporating the subject, that he made later in his career. He personally played the parts of law enforcement officers, and it is interesting to note that it was his film *The Detective* that marked the end of his short-lived marriage to Mia Farrow.

*   *   *

Coupled with the guilt he felt over the separation from his wife, Dickens's parental obligations now weighed heavily upon him. Among his children, it was only his son Harry who never gave him trouble. Walking together one day, the boy proudly told Dickens that he had won a scholarship to Cambridge University, and was disappointed when his father said nothing. When Harry turned and faced him, he saw that there were tears in his father's eyes. Dickens composed himself, turned to Harry and uttered "Capital! Capital!"

After so many disappointments, Dickens had become self-restrained in whatever moved him deeply, his intense feelings cutting him off from those he truly loved. Only when his children were little could he allow himself to be affectionate. Gone from home a great deal, his absences were more conspicuous because he was so full of life and fun when he was present. Throwing lavish children's parties, organizing home theatricals, performing magic tricks or taking his children to the store and personally helping them each chose the right toy, Dickens was always compensating for the time he spent away from his family and they adored him.

While Dickens didn't bond well with his sons, he had two daughters to whom he was very close. It was his second daughter (the third child) who was said to be the one most like him. Dickens would later bring two of his sons, Charlie and Frank, in to work with him as part of his magazine staff.

When his eldest child Charlie was a teenaged student at Eton, his father picked him up from school along with a group of his classmates, and took them out on a boat excursion on the river Thames. Charlie would be the first to marry and would present Dickens with his first grandchild, a girl, who they named *Mary Angela*.

*   *   *

Skipping ahead about a hundred years, the pattern of Dickens with his children repeats itself in the life of Frank Sinatra. Sinatra also felt a lot of guilt over leaving his first wife and his children. His daughter Tina claims in her book that her father was gripped by an intensity of feeling that cut him off from those he truly loved. Living apart from his children, Sinatra's absences were more conspicuous because he was so full of life and fun when he was there. Always organizing things to do with his kids, even if it was just taking them to the store to pick out a toy, Sinatra tried hard to compensate for the time he spent away from his family and they adored him.

Sinatra also had two daughters to whom he was very close to, and it is said that his second daughter (the third child) was the one most like him. He didn't bond as well with his son, Frank, but later on would bring him to work with him as his orchestra conductor.

When his eldest daughter Nancy was a teenager in high school, Sinatra once picked her up, along with a group of her classmates, and took them all on an excursion in his big Cadillac convertible. Nancy would be the first to marry and present Sinatra with his first grandchild, a girl, who they named *Angela*.

*   *   *

Dickens first faced his own mortality as his father lay dying. Staying by his father's bedside until the end, Dickens openly displayed great affection for him. After his father died, his mother gradually sank into senility; however, when Dickens would enter the room, she'd always pluck up and ask him for money! Over the years, his parents caused Dickens a great deal of grief and humiliation by frequently being in debt and by borrowing money from his friends behind his back. While Dickens always had a soft spot for his father, he had a love-hate relationship with his mother.

Frank Sinatra also had a soft spot for his father and a love-hate relationship with his mother. She spent Sinatra's money freely and embarrassed him by borrowing money from his friends behind his back. Sinatra would also face his own mortality for the first time when his father lay dying. To read the description of Sinatra, openly displaying great affection for his father while keeping vigil over him on his deathbed, one can't help but remember reading how Charles Dickens had reacted openly affectionate towards his own dying father in the very same way.

* * *

All throughout his twelve year performing career, Dickens retained his popularity as an author as he continued to write serial novels. Some of the names, themes and characters he chose for these later novels can also be looked upon as symbols relating to this myth, and seem to point ahead to Frank Sinatra.

Among these is the famous story of the young man named Pip who had *Great Expectations*. Fortune came his way, but barely compensated for the unrequited love he felt for the beautiful, unattainable *Estella*, who had been adopted, through a lawyer in *Smithfield*, by a rich eccentric woman who had brought the girl up to break the heart of every man who loved her.

Some say that Dickens had his Estella in Ellen Ternan and was *a prisoner of love*. There's little doubt that Frank Sinatra had his Estella in Ava Gardner, who reportedly also came from a town named *Smithfield*, (in North Carolina). Ava denied being born there, but there is no denying that she is buried there. Actually born in Grabtown, outside of Smithfield, Ava died in London (which Smithfield is a part of). Charles Dickens himself couldn't have come up with more Dickensian-sounding names of towns for the two star-crossed lovers of the most influential love affair of the twentieth century to be born in than Hoboken and Grabtown!!

Ava Gardner would one day shun Hollywood and eventually settle in London where the fictional Estella had resided. Her balconied flat overlooked a beautiful Victorian garden, which was planted in 1870, the year that Charles Dickens died. *How little we know* but that in the darkness of the barren soil of that London Square a garden was planted and was timed to bloom to its full glory for Frank's Estella when she finally settled there a century later. An ornamental urn now sits in that garden, commemorating the seventeen years Ava Gardner had lived there.

Charles Dickens had *great expectations* and Frank Sinatra had *high hopes!* The very last song that Sinatra sang in public was "The Best Is Yet To Come," the title of which is inscribed on his tombstone and which indicates that Frank Sinatra had *great expectations* too!!

Dickens set his historical novel, *A Tale of Two Cities,* in two different metropolitan cities, and the story concerns *two men who are very similar.* A young girl named Amy finds love in *Little Dorrit,* when her beloved finally realizes that "Once In Love With Amy," he'd always be in love with Amy. The song about Amy that Sinatra recorded is from the Broadway musical *Where's Charlie?"*

Two laughing children at play, Davy Copperfield and *Emily,* fall in love among the coral shells on the beach. In Dickens's last two complete novels, *Hard Times* has a circus setting, a scene probably not far removed from the one Harry James grew up in fifty years later, and Our *Mutual Friend* is the a story of a man with two identities, as well as another man who covered the waterfront in search of his love.

The characters Dickens created and wove into his myths also reinvented themselves, in time, into real life characters and themes in popular music; which is totally in sync with the very nature of myth in the first place.

*　　*　　*

Having finally found contentment in a relationship, Dickens would have loved to have married his blond ex-showgirl, Ellen Ternan, but had to settle for spending the last twelve years of his life with her in secret. Frank Sinatra would marry his ex-showgirl, Barbara Marx, and in their twenty-two years together they would build the Dickens dream home for needy children in Palm Springs.

As successful a businessman as Charles Dickens was, Frank Sinatra also owned various film and television production companies that for some reason he named after towns and counties (Bristol, Canterbury, Dorchester, Essex and Sheffield) in Britain! Sinatra loved London and he worshipped there—not only Ava Gardner—but in an obscure little Catholic Church in Maiden Lane that is located diagonally across the street from Dickens's favorite restaurant and just a block away from the round building where Charles Dickens had his magazine offices.

*   *   *

As they grew older, both men became increasingly more powerful. It is said that when Frank Sinatra walked into a crowded room, everyone virtually froze and all eyes turned to him. The same was said of Charles Dickens. People were continually struck by the brilliance and vitality of their eyes. Both men were obsessive about cleanliness and the clothes they wore, from the stylishness of their early clothing to the elegant seriousness of the evening dress they wore later in life. When Sinatra showed up at John F. Kennedy's Inaugural gala in 1961, dressed in a red satin-lined black Inverness cape, swallowtail coat, striped trousers, top hat and white gloves, it could well have been Dickens arriving for a similar event in 1861!

Queen Victoria herself has been said to remark to Dickens that she knew he was the most consistent of men. Everything in his household always had to be in its place and he would see to it personally that his children's rooms would be no exception. Sinatra too was said to remark "I am a symmetrical man, almost to a fault, I demand everything it its place", and he actively encouraged this trait in his children.

*   *   *

In a book she wrote about her father, Dickens's eldest daughter tells us that he was intensely fond of music and that she always regretted that he never cultivated singing, for he had a sweet voice and a perfect ear. Dickens was very critical as to the proper and distinct pronunciation of words in singing. While he enjoyed opera and classical music, romantic songs and good dance music were his favorites. He always enjoyed singing, listening to or playing music, despite the *inner ear damage* he had sustained after being in a train accident.

As a young man also intensely fond of music, with a sweet voice and a perfect ear, Frank Sinatra became famous for his proper and distinct pronunciation of words while singing. Despite having some elusive inner ear damage, he enjoyed listening to opera and classical music, but romantic songs and good dance music were his favorites. Always singing his signature song "I've Got You Under My Skin," one has to wonder who it was that was so deep in Frank Sinatra's heart and nearly a part of him?

9

BRAZIL

By this time of their lives, Charles Dickens and Frank Sinatra were both in their fifties, each having reached the pinnacle of their artistic career. What lay ahead for them was a continuation of their phenomenal careers as performing artists. Dickens would say that he knew what it was to have power when the thousands of the people in his audience were like one in their enthusiasm for him. He somehow knew, as did Sinatra, how to connect with each and every person in the audience in an intimate way and hold them in the palm of his hand. Frank Sinatra, taking it a huge step further, proved that the number of people in the audience was irrelevant when he performed in the biggest stadium in the world, in Rio de Janeiro, in front of almost two hundred thousand people, in what was then the biggest one-man show in history, with exactly the same effect!

It had taken forty years for Frank Sinatra to perform in Rio. His coming there was so long anticipated that it had become a long-standing joke among men to put off commitments to women by promising to marry them, or have a baby, only when Frank Sinatra came to Brazil!

So it was that on January 26, 1980, tens of thousands of people sat in their seats all day long in the pouring rain waiting for Frank Sinatra to perform that evening. Walking the considerable distance to center stage in that same pouring rain put the sixty-five year old singer out of breath. When he finally reached for the microphone, the rain miraculously stopped that instant! Sinatra paused, looked to the sky and offered a prayer of thanks to the Almighty. The applause that accompanied this spontaneous act of reverence was deafening, and when it finally ended Frank Sinatra started to sing in his own inimitable way to the largest audience that one man had ever performed in front of before. It was only when the singer faltered in the middle of singing "Strangers in the Night" that he gave the audience a chance to reciprocate. Forgetting the words in the middle of the song, two hundred thousand people sang them back to him! Triumphant, and still dry, Sinatra ended this monumental concert by putting the microphone down and, at that precise moment, it immediately started pouring rain again!

All things, they say, happen in their proper time. The oversight on the part of Sinatra and his managers in holding off for forty years the scheduling of his first performance in Brazil, a country geographically close to this one, is particularly suspicious in the light of Sinatra's performing as far away as Australia, not just once but twice in the 1950's.

The scheduling of that concert in Rio may have had to wait for all those collective souls to come together to pay homage to the now completed mission of this one man who, in the course of the twentieth century, had revolutionized popular music. This homage may also have been a tribute to the generative power of Charles Dickens who came before Sinatra. The audience may have been *strangers in the night* indeed, as the Myth now moved closer to coming full circle in Rio de Janeiro, the place where Charles Dickens's social conscience had its roots in the depths of the sea, where his uncle, the naval lieutenant, had drowned one hundred and fifty years before. Having been on this earth the century before, those souls may have vowed they would return, as the song says, to old *Brazil.*

*   *   *

What had happened to Frank Sinatra in Rio de Janeiro would repeat itself once more in the very same stadium, exactly ten years later in 1990, when the same size crowd greeted Paul McCartney of The Beatles. Almost thirty years after what has been called "The British Invasion" in popular music, no one had forgotten the now defunct rock group, hailing from *Liverpool,* who had taken America and the world by storm and caused a cultural revolution.

Coincidentally, it was in 1942, the same year teenagers began swooning over Frank Sinatra, that Paul McCartney was born in Liverpool. A corresponding coincidence is that Frank Sinatra was born in what is referred to as "The American Liverpool," Hoboken, New Jersey. Tying Dickens into the picture is the fact that Liverpool is the city he left from to sail to America on his own "British Invasion," in 1842, on one of the first transatlantic steamships, *The Britannia.* Bringing the myth round in a circle is the fact that the Beatles' Museum in Liverpool today is located at Britannia Pavilion, named after the great ship that brought Dickens here in the first place!

The Beatles rose to fame in gimmicky dress, looking like English schoolboys right out of a Dickens novel, when the pandemonium broke out on The Ed Sullivan Show on February 9. This is the very same date that the English schoolboy, Charles Dickens, first went to work in the blacking factory, an experience that was to have a profound effect on him, as well as the entire industrialized world. (February 9 was also the same date that Harry James, prior to discovering Frank Sinatra, had debuted his new orchestra on the very same spot in Philadelphia where Charles Dickens had stayed while visiting there.)

The Beatles were still forming as a group in England in 1962 when they hired *Ringo.* Frank Sinatra was also in England in June of that year, performing on his World Tour for Children and recording the album *Frank Sinatra Sings Great Songs From Great Britain* with Robert Farnon, whose Orchestra had represented Canada in World War II. The London recording studio was so packed with guests that day, that Sinatra invited people to sit surrounding him on the floor while he sang, just as Dickens often did.

With this tribute album to Britain, the Great War, and the British people, in whose lives at that perilous time The Voice had played an integral part, Frank Sinatra had come full circle with this significant part of his life's mission accomplished. It was now time to pass the torch of the evolutionary process of popular music, as a worldwide panacea, on to the Beatles, whose music would relate to and influence a whole new generation, once again emphasizing the potent reminder that *all you need is love!*

*　　*　　*

The origin of the name chosen for the phenomenon that became known as *The Beatles* is obscure. John Lennon's reply to the oft-asked question was that, at the age of twelve, it came to him in a vision. A man appeared in a flaming pie and informed him "From this day on you are Beatles with an A." True or not, this story has become a fascinating part of the Beatles myth lore.

One wonders if the Beatles ever took into consideration the fact that their name first became famous (or rather infamous) a century before when Charles Dickens exposed the Beadles to the world in his novel *Oliver Twist,* and that the man in Lennon's dream may very well have been Bumble himself, encrusted for eternity in the symbol of desire of so many starving children, just as Jacob Marley had been eternally chained to his cash box!

Arriving on the scene, the Beatles themselves each seemed to represent one of the fictional young heroes in Dickens's early novels. Paul McCartney with a face as innocent as David Copperfield, who finds lasting love and a soul mate in Agnes Wickfield, had also found the same in Linda Eastman. Myth has it that she was part of the Eastman family (of Eastman-Kodak) from Rochester. True or not, this story indirectly links Paul McCartney with the name of the place in England that Dickens considered his hometown.

(Strangely enough, Dickens's lasting love, Ellen Ternan was born in his hometown of Rochester and is buried in Dickens's birthplace, Portsmouth, along with his first love, Maria Beadnell, who lies in rest at the very same cemetery there!)

*　　*　　*

Exhausted after five years of fame and non-stop singing, The Beatles take off for a religious retreat in India and who should they meet up with there but the recently divorced Mia Farrow, Frank Sinatra's Ellen Ternan! This historic summit, in which the East met the West, would have a profound effect on the Beatles as well as the world. From then on the Western world would slowly begin to merge Eastern thought into our Western thinking, bringing us closer to a better understanding of life and the workings of the Universe.

What happened to the Beatles in America on February 9, 1964, on the 140th anniversary of Dickens's first day on the job at the blacking factory (February 9, 1824), and just two years after Sinatra's visit to Britain, is testimony to the fact that there was an exchange of a vast universal energy that had accumulated and somehow connected itself to this obscure British rock group from Liverpool making them immortal too!

*   *   *

In 1993, the year before he retired, Frank Sinatra, unaware that destiny itself may have been beckoning him, decided to perform for the very first time in Rochester, New York, a city where his multitude of fans had all but given up hope of ever seeing him there. Even Charles Dickens had performed in this namesake of his hometown in England in March 1868. Now Sinatra's time had come and what was waiting for him in Rochester was a reception quite unlike anything he had ever experienced before; the same type of reception that had greeted Dickens almost everywhere he went in the United States.

The rumor alone that Frank Sinatra would appear in Rochester was announced on every local television news station there and caused frenzy. Initially, there was widespread disbelief, as his visit was such a long time coming, and when the rumor was finally confirmed, the general anxiety was that Sinatra would cancel. What followed was one of the most exciting nights in Rochester's history. Newscasters announced that Frank Sinatra's performance was being billed as "a historic event." One newspaper reporter went so far as to say, "If it were not a fact that Hoboken was written on Frank Sinatra's birth certificate, one would think that Rochester was his hometown!"

Rochester was a bustling place the night of Sinatra's concert, with charity benefits being held at all of the upscale restaurants, and other eateries in the city featuring special Sinatra menus. Young fans dressed in *Pal Joey* suits and fedora hats compared record album covers, photographs, and other memorabilia, while others in rented limos all waited at the airport for Sinatra's flight to arrive. When he finally stepped out of the plane with his entourage everyone went wild! As his limo drove by the crowd on its way to the Concert, Sinatra opened the car window, reached out and slapped hands with some of the screaming fans who were standing by to greet him, giving them a glimpse of that marvelous tanned face and those incredible "blue as the sky" eyes.

Meanwhile, back in the center of town, people were hanging out of the windows of office buildings hoping to get a glimpse of Frank Sinatra when he arrived. Again, he didn't disappoint when he stepped out of the limo for a minute and waved to the cheering crowd. The city of Rochester had literally rolled out the red carpet to greet Sinatra, for when he arrived at the War Memorial Stadium, bright red carpets had been newly laid down on the sidewalks outside the building, as well as on the main floor of the arena. The ushers were also specially dressed in red suits for the occasion and hundreds of floral spreads, sent by fans, graced the floor around the arena. This was the grandest reception Rochester had ever given for any one celebrity. It was also one of the grandest receptions that Sinatra had ever received in any town in his entire six-decade career!

Appropriately, the singer would perform in the round that evening, but backstage, before the show began, Frank Sinatra was presented with a commemorative plaque with four *trains* on it, as a gift from local *Industry*. Moved to tears by the gesture, the singer promised to put on one hell of a show for them that night!

The lights went down, pandemonium built, and the audience gasped when they finally spotted Sinatra's now silver head approaching the stage set up for him in the stadium that night. Jumping from their seats, the fans cheers rose to a roar, and the emotion in the crowd, who had been waiting for this moment for so many years, seemed to explode. Waiting for the commotion to calm down, Sinatra finally broke into "Come Fly With Me," and the audience did just that as he maneuvered the audio flight and gave one of his best performances in many years. The show ended triumphantly with Sinatra waving to the crowd, assuring them that he would be coming back soon to set foot on that very same stage again. Everyone present wanted to believe that what he said was true, but in their hearts they knew that it would never be.

This historic performance at the War Memorial in Rochester, in April of 1993, with its inclusion of a presentation representing the two great symbols of the nineteenth century—trains and industry—would be one of the outstanding triumphs of Frank Sinatra's career. What awaited him was his last achievement as a recording artist: his *Duets* albums, made three months later on the Capitol label. Having lived his life with great passion and drama, the universe was now following suit in the same fashion, and was pulling Frank Sinatra along in a circle to complete the last cycle of his life and phenomenal career. The man, whose voice was a war memorial in itself, had come a long way, and it would be at this performance in the round in Rochester that he would touch base one last time with the energy generated by Charles Dickens, which he had already passed on to Paul McCartney and The Beatles.

10

THE LAST DANCE

When Dickens left America for the last time the journey home took nine days from the time he left New York until he arrived back in Liverpool, England. He had spent the sea voyage thinking about what he would be doing the rest of his life. The American tour had been hard on him; his tremendous energy had abated, he walked slower, his bright eyes were dimmed and he was having vision problems. Realizing it was nearing the time to call it quits, he decided to do a series of Farewell Readings in Britain, after which he would "read no more." While not a greedy man, Dickens constantly worried about the needs of his family. These last reading performances would give him the opportunity to earn a lot of money in a short period of time

Dickens was also very depressed at the departure of his youngest son to join his brother in Australia. If his health had been better, he would have loved to take advantage of the profitable, long-standing offer to read there and visit his sons at the same time. Preparing for the Farewell Readings in Britain was a distraction sorely needed by Dickens to get his mind off the sad parting. His performances, a triumph in every town, were completely sold-out. At times, when they were oversold, Dickens would invite some of the ladies in the audience to come up on to the stage with him, where they would sit at his feet on the floor surrounding him as he performed.

Dickens was determined to give the audiences something to remember him by and, after much deliberation, he came up with the very thing that would create a sensation. He would read from *Oliver Twist*, and reenact the murder of Nancy by Bill Sikes.

Carefully adapting the text, he rehearsed it over and over again until, with great acting skill, Charles Dickens "murdered" the imaginary Nancy with one ferocious blow after another. The result was so spellbinding that he had to consider whether it was possibly too horrifying for the public. There was only one way to determine if the piece was suitable for reading publicly and that was by having an invitation-only, sneak preview performance for select members of the press, as well as theatrical and literary people whose judgment Dickens could rely on.

On the night of the performance, the stage set consisted of a back panel with a dark screen on each side, with Dickens's solitary figure in the center, his every action clearly visible under the light of the gas lamps. As he read, the audience silently followed Nancy on the London Bridge as she made her way home, slowly approaching her fate. They watched in horror as Sikes brought down a heavy club and struck her again and again and then disappeared into the darkness. Everyone sat speechless at the abrupt conclusion and before they had a chance to whimper the set was whisked away, revealing a long table with bottles of champagne, trays of oysters, and waiters standing by to open and serve them. Dickens reappeared and graciously invited the audience to join him on the platform for refreshments. It was reported that the scene, with all of the exquisitely dressed ladies glimmering under the gaslight, resembled a garden of flowers that was laced with sparkling jewels.

Charles Dickens definitely knew how to do things with flair! The Nancy reading was a sensation and once the word was out people arrived in droves to see it. Audiences were virtually frozen in their seats and, at various times during performances, swooning young ladies would be carried out stiff and rigid.

The intensity of Dickens's performance, however, was taking a toll on his health. In Edinburgh Dickens acted out the scene so ferociously that he lost his breath as he was leaving the stage, collapsing into the arms of his manager, who had to support him to his dressing-room couch. His poor health now forced Dickens to cancel the last leg of his Farewell Tour and return to London for the final readings. By this time, however, he was so ill that he required his doctor, *Frank* Beard, to be present back stage at every performance. Dazed and worn, his appearance shocked his friends and family. His peripheral vision was affected, making it difficult for him to read signs; his left hand and arm felt strange and he was having trouble articulating. Dickens convinced himself that these were side effects of the medication he was taking but, instinctively, he knew that his life on the road was at an end.

*   *   *

The Final Farewell Reading, on the 15th of March *1870*, at St. James Hall in London was the shining hour of Charles Dickens's performing career. He walked out onto the stage, book in hand, at precisely eight o'clock, as an idolatrous audience rose to their feet and greeted him with cheers. Opening the book, he stood there smiling and waited to begin. He didn't close the book again until the Readings were over forever!

The cheers and applause seemed like they would never die down, but when they finally did Dickens cried as he spoke of the painful feelings with which he closed this episode of his life. With the haunting intonation of the words, "from these garish lights I vanish now forevermore," Dickens hoped the audience would *excuse him while he disappeared!*

*   *   *

It was in *1970* that Frank Sinatra also began to entertain thoughts of retiring from his performing career. He too was tired and in desperate need of a break. The final curtain came in 1971 when Sinatra closed his Farewell Concert with some highly emotional words, remarking that as he had started out as a saloon singer, he would end quietly by singing a saloon song. Journalist *Tommy* Thompson, writing about the Concert in an article for *Life* Magazine, described Sinatra quietly slipping from his words into singing "Angel Eyes." He had ordered the stage dressed in darkness, a pin spot picking out his profile in silhouette. He lit a cigarette and the smoke enveloped him while he ended the song with the last words "'Scuse me while I disappear", and he did just that! Thompson stated that it was the single most stunning moment he had ever witnessed on stage. He obviously wasn't around to see Charles Dickens's Farewell Performance the century before, but Dickens's oldest friend—journalist *Tommy* Beard—probably was.

Frank Sinatra definitely knew how to do things with flair too! Once more he followed a pattern set by Charles Dickens, who also started his performing career as a saloon singer. Sinatra had tried retiring from that performing career around the same age and in the very same style as Dickens. Fortunately, for all of us and for Sinatra, it didn't work this time!

*   *   *

It wasn't very long before Sinatra began to realize that there was a whole new world of fans out there to conquer and in two years he announced that Ol' Blue Eyes was back! In 1973, he came out of retirement with a spectacular concert in Madison Square Garden, in New York, called "The Main Event." Despite waning vocal power, Sinatra was once more able to reinvent himself by relating to a new generation of fans with his inimitable power of self-expression, faultless phrasing and timing. He began to rely on and use more of his skills as an actor, as Charles Dickens had done in his readings, to more convincingly accentuate the words of the songs he was performing. While singing his classic tune, "The Lady Is A Tramp," Sinatra turned to the orchestra in the middle of the song and raising his fist, he conducted four blows toward them expounding the forceful word, "pow, pow, pow, pow". Frank Sinatra seemed to be killing that lady who was a tramp all over again!

*   *   *

Unlike Dickens, who lived less than 3 months after retiring, Frank Sinatra would have almost 30 years to live after he retired the first time. The accounts of their last performances on stage are hauntingly similar. Sinatra, as dazed and worn as Dickens, also had problems with articulating and with his peripheral vision. He had trouble reading the teleprompter and was at a loss to remember the words to familiar songs. His eye and hand coordination was affected also. This may have been a side effect of the medication he was taking but as with Charles Dickens, age and failing health did not impede his determination to go on.

Toward the end of his life, Frank Sinatra also began to worry about the needs of his family and pushed himself to perform longer than he should have in order to earn more money. Unlike Dickens, he was never forced to restrict where his performances would take place and traveled as far as Japan for one of his last concerts, just as he had traveled as far as Australia for one of his early ones! Dickens would have given a great deal to be able to have gone to Australia to perform and at the same time visit his two sons living there, who he would never see again. It was love also that drew Sinatra to Australia in the fifties, in spite of the many inconveniences of the early days of transoceanic flights. Following his muse, Ava Gardner, brought Sinatra to the place that Dickens was unable to get to!

*   *   *

It was a long way down the road until Sinatra would retire again and this time it would be entirely against his will. During one of his last performances in Atlantic City, Frank Sinatra stood on the stage and cried, just as Charles Dickens had cried across that same ocean, at his last performance in London, the century before.

A century and the Atlantic Ocean—the two primary symbols that paradoxically separate as well as connect these two men and their remarkable lives to each other and serve to remind us that the influence of great spirits can bridge centuries as well as oceans.

11

SOFTLY, AS I LEAVE YOU

In the end it was ill health that finally forced Charles Dickens to retire from his performing career. From the time he was a child he had suffered from debilitating kidney spasms that sometimes sent him reeling to the floor. Lifelong high blood pressure may have been the physiological effect that contributed to the enormous creativity and restless energy he experienced all of his life and which burnt him out early in the end. A train accident he was in on June 9, 1865 left him with inner ear damage and shattered nerves. Exactly five years later, on the very same day (June 9) as the train wreck, Dickens died of a stroke. He was fifty-eight years old.

It had been just three months since Dickens, at his doctor's orders, retired from the stage. His poor health necessitated that his physician friend *Frank* Beard stand by while he was performing. Frank was with him at Gad's Hill as he lay dying, and was also among the few people closest to Dickens who were invited to attend his private funeral and burial in Westminster Abbey. For the thousands of people who had come to pay tribute, the grave was kept open days after the ceremony for them to pass by.

The unexpected news of Dickens's death had spread quickly. It was as overwhelming a shock in places as far away as India and Australia as it was in England. In Russia, Leo Tolstoy hung a picture of Dickens above his desk on the wall in his study. Longfellow wrote from America reporting that the whole country was stricken with grief. And in Genoa, Italy, on the day that their newspaper headline read "Carlo Dickens e' morto," the town people were saddened by the loss of a man they considered one of their own.

* * *

It was ill health also that finally forced Frank Sinatra to retire in the end. He too had an ailment that had plagued him since birth; one, in fact, that he had in common with Charles Dickens— inner ear damage—although Dickens acquired this later in life. This impairment may also have been the physiological effect that contributed to Sinatra's musical creativity since he had no formal training but could hear and do things with music that others couldn't. The auditory nerve leading to his brain may have been in some way impaired, causing some unusual unknown form of compensation that enhanced his musical perception.

Frank Sinatra died three years after he retired from performing. The news of his death spread quickly. His burial in Palm Springs, like Dickens's funeral in London, would be private. But now people all over the world could pay tribute to him for almost a week, as they watched the extended television coverage on his death and his funeral, interspersed with coverage of his phenomenal six-decade career. Once again, as in the war years, the young man singing with his arms outstretched embraced the whole world with love. Visually joining in the vigil outside the Church as his funeral mass took place, the world waited and then watched as the gardenia covered casket was carried out and lifted into the hearse, removing Frank Sinatra's physical presence from the public eye—after almost sixty years—for the very last time!

*　　*　　*

In the end—they say—is the beginning. Henry James was one of the last persons to leave an account of seeing Charles Dickens at a dinner party in Boston on his last visit there in 1867-68. James wasn't yet the famous novelist, he was still just young Harry, but he describes being in an intensely emotional state—trembling in every limb—when, as he put it, "I saw the Master."

In the century to follow, another Harry James would describe himself as being in a similar emotional state, when he recognized "The Master" the very first time he saw and heard Frank Sinatra singing.

And, with that, the first encounter with "The Voice" of the twentieth century was born, its essence rooted in "The Voice" of the century before, and brought to our attention by two men with a coincidental name!

EPILOGUE

OL' MAN RIVER

*T*he song is ended as far as the pop culture myth connecting Charles Dickens and Frank Sinatra leaves off. Under the surface, however, the melody is still lingering on. Peeling back the layers of the myth reveals the phenomenal backdrop of world changing events of the past two centuries, which enables us to compare this myth not only on the basis of the relationship between the two men involved, but on the basis of the genetic relationship between the two countries they lived in. This boundary type relationship comes about when a large society breaks off and another takes form from it. The new society will develop its own version of the same myth. Their myths are then said to have a genetic relationship, which is clearly evident of the United States's role in the twentieth century following Great Britain's in the nineteenth.

Britain's great sea battles had created the need for rapidly produced wood for ships and the industrial age was born. The need to transport industrial products rapidly sped up the invention of faster means of travel, enabling Dickens to more readily make the long sea journey across the Atlantic Ocean. To America the voice of the nineteenth century would go. In fact, Dickens came, he saw and he criticized everything he didn't like and what sickened him the most was the sight of slavery!

The twentieth century lay in wait for the time when America's myth would take prominence. The main issue of the century would be as historian-sociologist W.E.B. DuBois accurately predicted in 1900— "the color line." We know now that it was music that helped initiate healing the breach between black and white in America in the twentieth century. It was on this issue also that Frank Sinatra's thoughts and feelings were expressed in his outspokenness on the subject of race through the many long years of his fame.

One has only to pause and reflect to realize that in each case "The Voice" was given the unique gifts of genius, longevity of fame and a worldwide audience for more reason than one. The greatest novelist of all time and the greatest singer of all time each had another job to do, and that job did not entail silence. Mythically speaking, this is very likely the underlying reason they've each been labeled "The Voice".

WE'LL MEET AGAIN

I first noticed this comparison of Frank Sinatra with Charles Dickens back in 1970 while reading a biography of Dickens for the first time. Over the years, strange coincidences would crop up now and then to remind me of the unexplainable connection, but I never gave them much thought until the day after Frank Sinatra died in 1998.

The following information chronicles some of the subjects I had been studying during the course of that twenty-eight year gap which, unknowingly, were preparing me to finally understand that the connection between these two men was myth.

*   *   *

UNDERSTANDING THIS MYTH

Science tells us that the world is made up of atoms. We can live a thousand lifetimes and never realize this; yet we need no authority figure to tell us the unmistakable truth that what the world is really made up of are stories. These stories are called myths. Myths go back to the beginning of time and their reach is never-ending. Each and every one of us has a story and in that story, according to Carl Jung, lies the myth that we live by. Jung goes so far as to recommend that everyone know the myth they live by. How do we do this? We do this by going back and re-examining our lives and focusing on the little things. Why? Because it is the little things that helped to make the big things happen.

As you progress in this process of self-realization (a backward flowing), you begin to experience many strange coincidences that at first don't seem to mean anything. But according to *The Chinese Book of Life: The Secret of the Golden Flower,* these coincidences are actually confirmatory experiences and a way that the Cosmos communicates with us. For example, if you have an insight into an experience, which is unobservable to anyone but yourself, it is usually followed by a coincidence that directly relates to the subject of the insight. This coincidence confirms that you are irrevocably correct. If you're still not convinced, you simply wait with awareness and do nothing—this is called "wu wei" in Chinese, which means "action in non-action." The truth will eventually reveal itself in a cluster of coincidences (representing the blooming of the Golden Flower and its many petals) that appear in your life simultaneously, incorporating various, seemingly unrelated aspects of your myth into one experience.

This knowledge was handed down to us by Richard Wilhelm, a German Scholar, who had spent twenty years in China studying the culture there. The culmination of this lifetime of learning was the translation of the ancient Chinese text, *The Secret of the Golden Flower,* which he felt would be of immense value to the whole human race. Shortly after translating the Chinese text into German, Richard Wilhelm died. Fortunately, he had passed the torch of this acquired knowledge and wisdom on to Carl Jung, who wrote the Commentary for the first edition of Wilhelm's book, in an attempt to explain the strange but valuable text. Jung recognized the importance of integrating Eastern thought into our Western thinking in order to come to a more complete understanding of life. Through years of practicing his analytical psychology on hundreds of patients, Jung found that many of their lives followed a pattern similar to "the way of all life" described in the book's teachings, even though not one of these patients were Chinese. Like the subject of myth, *The Secret of the Golden Flower* still lies in the mystery of silence, waiting for the time to come when its truth can be understood by all.

Fifty years after *The Secret of the Golden Flower* was first published in the western world, PBS aired a six-hour television series called *The Power of Myth,* in which journalist Bill Moyers interviewed Joseph Campell, the world-famous Mythologist. Campbell had spent nearly a half-century teaching people about myths by weaving fascinating ancient stories with eternal truths. An Octogenarian by this time, Campbell, with the help of the latest technology in broadcasting, was able to pass on some of this valuable knowledge, which took a lifetime to acquire, to the whole world in a matter of hours. His mission obviously complete, Joseph Campbell, like Richard Wilhelm, died shortly thereafter.

Basically, what Campbell taught is that we are living the same myths (or stories) that people lived before us and that from those myths new myths are created over and over again. In other words, myths reinvent themselves. Myths are common to all mankind; they are universal and have no boundaries. Because a story is called a myth doesn't mean that it never happened. A myth is merely a story that has been brought down to us through the ages, and while it may have incurred some change along the way, its elementary truth remains the same. Myths help us to understand why people behave as they do. They are guideposts that show us how to live and help us to gain knowledge that is not easily acquired elsewhere.

The key ingredient to understanding myth is comprehending symbols. Symbols are vehicles of communication that assist our understanding. A symbol differs from a sign in that a sign represents one thing, whereas a symbol incorporates many things. Symbols must be interpreted and assembled for a coherent picture to emerge and this process involves waiting. This book is a direct result of that process.

Name and number symbolisms are important in myths. Names reveal the nature of things and connect them to each other. Coincidental names often show up in our lives and sometimes run through them like a thread. In his sixth dialogue, Plato discusses name symbology with Cratylus. Though nothing was proven, or even agreed upon, it's doubtful that Plato would have been discussing the subject if there weren't more to names than meets the eye. A surprising number of coincidental names link Frank Sinatra with Charles Dickens in this story of a shared myth. This is a direct device that the Cosmos uses in an attempt to capture our attention.

Numbers are even more mysterious symbols. Everything, they say, lies veiled in numbers ("Omnia in numeris sita sunt"). Numbers represent the self, as well as cycles and stages of growth and development. The question is, does this growth and development extend beyond one lifetime? More than we ever realize, coincidental numbers and dates permeate our lives as we move through the cycles of our time here on earth.

Also to be taken into consideration when attempting to understand this particular myth is the universal law of moral cause and effect called Karma, that governs the physical world and possibly rebirth. Karma teaches that what you are today is a result of your past, and this could very well also mean a past life. A fortifying aspect of this, and one that seems quite evident in this myth, would be Ralph Waldo Emerson's theory *On Compensation*, which states that nothing can be given to us or taken away from us without our receiving compensation. Frank Sinatra's relationship to Charles Dickens in this myth often appears suspiciously compensatory.

G.K. Chesterton's description of Dickens as "a naked flame of mere natural genius" applies to Sinatra as well, and gives credence to the axiom "a man possesses talent, but genius possesses the man." Talent was in the genes of their heredity; the mystery is where did their genius come from? Carl Jung, in his theory of the collective unconscious, details a level of consciousness that is shared by the whole human race, which points to an inherited type of psychic genes that have nothing to do with our biological background. Evidence of this is the fact that a man's genius is usually not inherited from his antecedents, shared by his siblings or passed on to his children.

This theory brings us to the first and second law of thermodynamics, the Principal of Equivalence and the Principal of Entropy, which Jung felt also applied to psychic energy. This involves the balance of the energy generated and the direction of the flow. Charles Dickens, born at the same time that the industrial revolution was fueling up, was one of the most energetic and industrious men who ever lived. Perpetually in motion and prodigiously productive, Dickens was a human machine. He was a great generator of power: a mighty eagle.

Traveling is the most crucial aspect in myth transference. We have to travel in order to touch base to connect with someone else for the transference of energy. To put it simply, I call this "passing the torch", although it is a quite a bit more complex than this. The only subject to offer an analogy to help understand this theory on the importance of traveling for energy transference is the study of the effects of planetary transits in our lives, as they relate to the natal horoscope in Astrology. To go into anymore detail would entail my writing another book on the subject.

Over the centuries, the means of travel has advanced from coach, boat, train and airplane to spacecraft. These forms of transport are all symbols that take us where we must go to do the work of the Master. In time they all change; only the myth remains the same.

A perfect example of the importance of traveling in myth is the story of Jesus where the angel appears to His mother Mary. The first thing Mary does after receiving the glad tidings is to travel. With Child in womb, Mary immediately goes off to visit her cousin Elizabeth, who is carrying John the Baptist, the one who is to go before Christ. The night Mary's Child is born she's on the road again looking for a place to stay; and after Jesus is born, the Holy Family flees into Egypt. Jesus has his first awakening at the Temple in Jerusalem after journeying there with his parents. Later, Jesus traveled and met up with his cousin John, who baptized Him as an initiation into the mission in life that awaited Him. All of His earthly life, Jesus continually moved around in the greatest myth of all time in order to allow things to happen.

Charles Dickens and Frank Sinatra also moved around a great deal in their myths. Their families didn't get to see a whole lot of them, but as Christ said, a man sometimes has to leave his family to follow Him. He didn't mean literally to follow Him, but to follow His example. Jesus came to save the world in His own way, and in different ways through their art, so did Charles Dickens and Frank Sinatra. If Sinatra was indeed initiated into the mission that awaited him on his baptismal day, the fact that the ceremony was held on Dickens's wedding anniversary points to his possibly being a psychic (or spiritual) descendant of Dickens, which certainly isn't incompatible with this theory that they lived the same myth. The many parallels in their lives also confirm this and it seems ludicrous to think of anyone living Dickens's myth without his trademark: coincidences.

The question is, however, was it more than myth? Was it also reincarnation? With the increasing interest today in the subject of reincarnation, and with many people claiming they were someone else, somewhere else, in other lifetimes, it's hard to ignore the two most visible men of the past two centuries, because Charles Dickens and Frank Sinatra were on display for practically their whole adult lifetimes. Their lives were an open book. Countless numbers of words have been written about each of them, and to this day it hasn't stopped, as people still thirst for knowledge about every aspect of their fabulous lives. I challenge anyone who claims they were someone else in a different lifetime to come up with more evidence than is apparent in these two life stories. Was Frank Sinatra Charles Dickens? That you must decide for yourself.

If the connection between Dickens and Sinatra is a myth, then the myth must necessarily have a source. In view of this, let us consider the following story, which has been adapted from an old American Indian myth:

THE EAGLE AND THE LARK
A LEGEND

There once was a mighty eagle who soared so high in the sky that he could reach the domain of the gods. Embarrassed by his gruff earthy voice, the eagle never dared to call out to the gods even though he desired their attention in order to show them all that he had achieved with the powerful gift they had given him at birth.

One day a little lark looked on admiringly as the mighty eagle soared high into the sky. The lark waited long into the darkness of the night for the eagle to land, and when he finally did, the tiny lark bravely approached the great bird to explain his dilemma. The lark, who was renowned for his beautiful singing, told the eagle that he would sing from dawn to dusk, but the more he sang, the more the feelings of desire would well up in his breast to sing for the gods. If only he could fly high enough into the sky, the gods would be sure to hear him and be pleased with what he had done with the gift they given him at birth. Plucking up his courage, the little lark then asked the mighty eagle to carry him on his back so that, with the eagle's immense power and his grandiose voice, together they could offer the fruit of their gifts to entertain the gods.

With great eagerness the eagle agreed to the lark's request and the little bird climbed up onto his back. As the eagle ascended higher and higher, he carried the lark to greater heights than he had ever dreamed of. Looking down onto the earth below, the tiny bird became frightened. But his fears abided as they reached the heavenly realm and the lark suddenly felt empowered as he realized his destiny. Filling his lungs with air, the lark stood tall on the eagle's back and filled the Heavens with the same magnificent sounds that he had been born to grace the earth with. The gods, amazed at the mighty power of the eagle and enthralled by the exquisite beauty of the lark's song, sent blessings back with them to the earth below. As a team, together, the eagle and the lark had brought the music of the earthly sphere to the Heavens to honor the gods above.

Many a songbird may sing but only one found the way to reach the gods by riding on the back of the eagle.

BIBLIOGRAPHY

BOOKS

Ackroyd, Peter. *Dickens.* New York: HarperCollins, 1990.

Brady, Bernadette. *Predictive Astrology: The Eagle and the Lark.* York Beach, Maine: Samuel Weiser, Inc. 1992

Campbell, Joseph. *The Hero With A Thousand Faces.* Princeton: Princeton University Press, 1973.

_____*Myths to Live By.* New York: Viking Penguin, 1993.

_____*The Power of Myth.* New York: Doubleday, 1988.

_____*Transformation of Myth Through Time.* New York: Harper & Row, 1990.

Campbell, Joseph. ed. *The Portable Jung.* New York: Viking Penguin, 1984.

Chesterton, G.K. *Charles Dickens: A Critical Study.* New York: Dodd Mead, 1920.

Coleman, Ray. *Sinatra: A Portrait of the Artist.* Atlanta: Turner Publishing, 1995.

Collins, Phillip, ed. *Dickens: Interviews and Recollections,* 2 vols. New Jersey: Barnes & Noble, 1981.

Dickens, Sir Henry Fielding. *Memories of My Father.* New York: Duffield & Co., 1929.

Dickens, Mamie. *My Father As I Recall Him.* London: The Roxburghe Press. n.d.

Dolby, George. *Charles Dickens As I Knew Him: The Story of The Reading Tours in Great Britain and America.* New York: Haskell House, 1970.

Farrow, Mia. *What Falls Away: A Memoir.* New York: Doubleday, 1997.

Gardner, Ava. *Ava: My Story.* New York: Bantam Books, 1990.

Granata, Charles L. *Sessions with Sinatra: Frank Sinatra and The Art of Recording.* Chicago: Independent Publishers Group, 1999.

Fido, Martin. *Charles Dickens: An Authentic Account of His Life & Times.* U.K.: Hamlyn Publishing Group, 1970.

_____*The World of Charles Dickens: The Life, times and works of the great Victorian novelist.* London: Carlton Books, 1997.

Fitzsimons, Raymund. *Garish Lights: The Public Reading Tours of Charles Dickens.* Philadelphia: J.B. Lippincott, 1970.

Forster, John. *The Life of Charles Dickens.* 2 vols. London: J.M. Dent & Sons, 1966.

Grudens, Richard. *Snootie Little Cutie: The Connie Haines Story.* Souix Falls, S.D. Pine Hill Press, Inc. 2000

Hamill, Pete. *Why Sinatra Matters.* New York: Little, Brown & Co., 1998.

House, Madeline, Graham Storey, Kathleen Tillotson, and K.J. Fielding, eds. *The Letters of Charles Dickens.* 12 vols. The Pilgrim Edition, Oxford, U.K.: The Clarendon Press, 1955.

Johnson, Edgar. *Charles Dickens: His Tragedy and Triumph.* 2 vols. New York: Simon & Schuster, 1952.

Jung, Carl G. *Man and His Symbols.* New York: Doubleday, 1983.

Kelley, Kitty. *His Way: The Unauthorized Biography of Frank Sinatra.* New York: Bantam Books, 1986.

Koestler, Frances A. *The Unseen Minority: A Social History of Blindness in the United States.* New York: David McKay, 1976.

Lahr, John. *Sinatra: The Artist And The Man.* New York: Random House, 1997.

Larsen, Stephen and Robin Larsen. *A Fire in the Mind: The Life of Joseph Campbell.* New York: Doubleday, 1991.

Leacock, Stephen. *Charles Dickens: His Life and Work.* New York: Doubleday, Doran & Co., 1936.

Levinson, Peter J. *Trumpet Blues: The Life of Harry James.* New York: Oxford University Press, 1999.

Mustazza, Leonard. *Ol' Blue Eyes: A Frank Sinatra Encyclopedia.* Westport, Ct.: Greenwood Press, 1998.

_____*Frank Sinatra and Popular Culture: Essays on an American Icon.* Westport, Ct.: Praeger Publishers, 1998.

Sinatra: An Annotated Bibliography, 1939-1998. Westport, Ct.: Greenwood Press, 1999.

The Frank Sinatra Reader. ed.Petkov, Steven & Mustazza, Leonard. New York: Oxford University Press. 1995

Nisbet, Ada. *Dickens and Ellen Ternan.* With a foreword by Edmund Wilson. Berkeley: University of California Press, 1952.

Plato. *Cratylus.* Translated by C.D.C. Reeve. Indianapolis: Hackett Publishing, 1998.

Pope-Hennesey, Una. *Charles Dickens.* London: Chatto and Windus, 1945. Reprinted London: The Reprint Society, 1947.

Rockwell, John. *Sinatra: An American Classic,* New York: Random House, 1984.

Schlicke, Paul. ed. *Oxford Reader's Companion to Dickens.* Oxford, U.K. Oxford University Press, 1999.

Sinatra, Nancy. *Frank Sinatra: My Father.* New York: Pocket Books, 1986.

_____*Frank Sinatra: an American Legend.* Santa Monica, Ca.: General Publishing Group,1995,1998.

Sinatra, Tina. Jeff Coplon. *My Father's Daughter: A Memoir.* New York: Simon & Schuster, Adult Publishing Group, 2000.

Slater, Michael. *Dickens on America & the Americans.* Austin and London: University of Texas Press, 1978.

Storey, Gladys. *Dickens and Daughter.* Manchester, U.K.: Frederick Muller Ltd., 1939.

Tomalin, Claire. *The Invisible Woman: The Story of Nelly Ternan and Charles Dickens.* New York: Alfred A. Knopf, 1991.

Taraborrelli, J. Randy. *Sinatra: Behind the Legend.* New Jersey: Carol Publishing 997.

Wilhelm, Richard. translator. *The Secret of The Golden Flower: A Chinese Book of Life.* With a Foreword and Commentary by Carl G. Jung. New York: Harcourt, Brace Jovanovich, 1962.

Wilkins, William Glyde. *Charles Dickens in America.* New York: Haskell House, 1970.

Wilson, Angus. *The World of Charles Dickens.* London: Martin Secker & Warburg.1970.

Zehme, Bill. *The Way You Wear Your Hat: Frank Sinatra and the Lost Art of Livin'.* New York: HarperCollins, 1997.

REFERENCE

"Mythology". *The World Book Encyclopedia.* Chicago: World-Book-Childcraft International, Inc. 1981

PERIODICALS

Down Beat. "Sinatra Flick on Intolerance a Fine Attempt". 1 November 1945

Entertainment Weekly. (Special Collector's Issue). "Sinatra: The Man, the Music, the Movies & the Women." Summer 1998: 80 pages.

Jet. "LA Branch of NAACP Give Sinatra Achievement Award". 1 June 1987: 56

Life Magazine. "Frank Sinatra in Gary". 12 November 1945. P.45-46

Life Magazine. (Special Commemorative Tribute Issue), "Remembering Sinatra: A Life in Pictures." ed. Robert Sullivan and the editors of *Life.* 1998: 128 pages.

People Magazine. (Tribute). "Frank Sinatra: His Life, His Way." May/June 1998: 80 pages.

ARTICLES

Bryson, John.   "Sinatra at Fifty." *Look.* 14 December 1965: 61-74.

Sinatra, Frank.   "The Haters and The Bigots Will Be Judged".
                   The Los Angeles Times. 4 July 1991: B5
                   "Let's Not Forget We're *All* Foreigners".
                   Magazine Digest. July 1945: 8
                   "Letter of the Week: As Sinatra Sees It".
                   The New Republic. 6 January 1947: 3,
                   46
                   "Me and My Music." *Life.* 23 April 1965:
                   86-87, 99-104.
                   "The Way I Look At Race". *Ebony.* July 1958
                   "What's This About Races". *Scholastic.* 17
                   September 1945: 23

Talese, Gay.   "Frank Sinatra Has A Cold." *Esquire.* April
                  1966: 89-98+.
                       Reprinted in *The Frank Sinatra Reader.*
                  Mustazza, Leonard. New York. Oxford
                  University Press. 1995

Thompson, Thomas. "Frank Sinatra's Swan Song." *Life.* 25 June
                  1971: 70A-74.
                       Reprinted in *The Frank Sinatra Reader.*
                  Mustazza, Leonard New York. Oxford
                  University Press. 1995

TELEVISION

Sinatra, Frank.   Interview with Edward R. Murrow. Aired 15
                  September 1956. Sinatra discusses relief fund
                  set up for retired actors.

Sinatra Frank.   *Sinatra: An American Original,* Narr. Walter
                  Cronkite. *CBS.* 16 November 1965. One hour
                  documentary, aired the month before Sinatra's
                  fiftieth birthday, Film chronicles six months
                  of his life and includes footage of his benefit
                  performance in a penitentiary.

Sinatra, Nancy.   *Movin' With Nancy.* Dir. Jack Haley, Jr. Aired
                  11 December 1967

FILM

Anchors Aweigh. Dir. George Sidney. MGM. 1945.
Can-Can. Dir. Walter Lang. Twentieth Century-Fox. 1960.
The Detective. Dir. Gordon Douglas. Twentieth Century-Fox. 1968.
Frank Sinatra and All God's Children. Shot in England.
                    Narr. Frank Sinatra. June 1962.
                    Twenty minute short featuring Sinatra,
                    along with members of the royal family,
                    visiting the Sunshine House Nursery School for
                    the Blind in Middlesex, London.
                    Never released to the media.
From Here to Eternity. Dir. Fred Zimmerman. Columbia. 1953.
The House I Live In. Dir. Mervyn LeRoy. RKO. 1945. Film short about
                    racial and religious tolerance. Star. Frank Sinatra.
The Miracle of The Bells. Dir. Irving Pichel. RKO. 1948.
Not As A Stranger. Dir. Stanley Kramer. United Artists. 1955.
On The Town. Dir. Stanley Donen and Gene Kelly. MGM. 1949.
One Touch of Venus. Dir. William Seiter. Republic Studios. 1948.
Ship Ahoy. Dir. Edward Buzzell. MGM. 1942.
Young At Heart. Dir. Gordon Douglas. Arwin/Warner Bros. 1955.

SONG TITLES

SONGS:	WRITTEN BY:
"All The Way"	Jimmy Van Heusen, Sammy Cahn & Lillian Small
"All You Need Is Love"	John Lennon & Paul Mc Cartney
"Angel Eyes"	Matt Dennis & Earl Brent
"Autumn in New York"	Vernon Duke
"Autumn Leaves"	Johnny Mercer
"Battle Hymn of the Republic"	Julia Ward Howe
"Baubles, Bangles and Beads"	George Forrest & Robert Wright
"The Best is Yet to Come"	Cy Coleman & Carolyn Leigh
"Beyond The Sea"	Charles Trent & Jack Lawrence

"Brazil"	Ary Barroso & S.K. Russell
"The Continental"	Con Conrad & Herb Magidson
"Don't Worry 'Bout Me"	Rube Bloom & Ted Koehler
"Emily"	Johnny Mandel & Johnny Mercer
"Fairy Tale"	Jerry Livingston & Dak Stanford
"A Foggy Day"	George & Ira Gershwin
"For Me And My Girl"	Geo W. Meyer
"From Here To Eternity"	Fred Karger & Robert Wells
"From This Moment On"	Cole Porter
"How Little We Know"	P. Springer & Carolyn Leigh
"High Hopes"	Jimmy Van Heusen & Sammy Cahn
"The House I live in"	Earl Robinson & Lewis Allan
"I Could Have Danced All Night"	Frederick Loewe & Alan Jay Lerner
"I Could Write A Book"	Lorenz Hart & Richard Rodgers
"I Cover the Waterfront"	Johnny Green & Edward Heyman
"I'm Walking Behind You"	Billy Reid
"In The Wee Small Hours of the Morning"	David Mann & Bob Hilliard
"I've Got The World On A String"	Harold Arlen & Ted Koehler
"I've Got You Under My Skin"	Cole Porter
"Just In Time"	Jule Styne, Betty Comden & Adolph Green
"Just One Of Those Things"	Cole Porter
"The Lady Is A Tramp"	Richard Rodgers & Lorenz Hart
"The Last Dance"	Jimmy Van Heusen & Sammy Cahn
"Laura"	David Raksin & Johnny Mercer
"London By Night"	Carroll Coates
"The Lonesome Road"	Gene Austin & Nathaniel Shilkret
"Mr. Success"	Ed Grienes, Hank Sanicola & Frank Sinatra
"My Shining Hour"	Harold Arlen & Johnny Mercer
"My Way "	Jaques Revaux, Claude Francois,

	Gilles Thibault & Paul Anka
"Nancy"	Jimmy Van Heusen & Phil Silvers
"Not As A Stranger"	Jimmy Van Heusen & Buddy Kaye
"Ol' Man River"	Jerome Kern & Oscar Hammerstein II
"Put Your Dreams Away"	Paul Mann, Stephan Weiss & Ruth Lowe
"Ring A Ding-Ding"	Jimmy Van Heusen & Sammy Cahn
"The Star-Spangled Banner"	Francis Scott Key
"Softly, As I Leave You"	A. DeVita, Gino Calabrese & Hal Shapiro
"The Song is Ended"	Irving Berlin
"Strangers In The Night"	Bert Kaempfert, Eddie Snyder & Charles Singleton
"We'll Meet Again"	Ross Parker & Hughie Charles
"Young At Heart"	Johnny Richards & Carolyn Leigh

ACKNOWLEDGMENTS

This story, and the insights therein, would not have been possible without the information that I've acquired through reading the books listed in the bibliography. My gratitude goes to the authors of these books for sharing their acquired knowledge and wisdom, thereby enhancing my perception of life's experiences.

My sincere thanks also go to the following family members, friends, and others who I have met along the way, who have provided me with the help, information or the inspiration that has assisted me in the writing of this book: The late Marjorie Pillers, former Curator of the Dickens House Museum in London and my confidant for twenty years. She introduced me to the rare photo of Charles Dickens that is seen on the cover of this book. The late Martha Rosso, Millie Casey and Lauren Vinci for proofreading and editing; Maria Vinci, Scott Vinci, Chris Duminiak and Vince Camiolo for technical help; singer Connie Haines, songwriter Ervin Drake, Ed Walters in Las Vegas, Gregg Dispenza and Maryann Mastrodonato in Rochester, N.Y., for sharing their personal stories about Frank Sinatra with me; Leonard Mustazza, PhD., Robert L. Patten, PhD., John J. Sweeder, PhD., Coleen Toews and Tom Walsh for ideas and inspiration; astrologer extraordinaire Bernadette Brady for passing on *The Fable of The Eagle and The Lark* in her book *Predictive Astrology*, and Salome/Wilhelm who haunted my dreams and waking and taught me *The Secret of The Golden Flower*.

My greatest debt, however, is to my teachers, Charles Dickens and Frank Sinatra. Through their art, they have helped form my whole mental attitude and have enhanced my own personal life experience in the process.